MW01170736

The Longest Goodbye

"The Strength of a Family's Love: A Caregiver's Journey"

By

Karyn Banner & Nicolette Banner

Contents

Dedication

In these pages, I dedicate not just the words that flow from my heart but every ounce of emotion that binds us together to my mother. You, my dear mother, were the pinnacle of strength that shaped me into the person I am today. With an unwavering resolve and an unyielding spirit, you guided me through the darkest storms and showed me the way to the shimmering light beyond.

Within your heart, I found solace in your words, wisdom, and actions, the embodiment of love. Your love, flowing endlessly like a gentle river, nourished my soul, and through every trial and tribulation, you remained steadfast, offering unwavering support and an unshakable belief in me.

This dedication extends beyond our relationship, paying homage to all those courageous souls who chose the caregiving path and to those who selflessly set aside their own lives and ambitions, tirelessly devoting themselves to the well-being of another.

In this modern world, where individualism sometimes overshadows our humanity, caregivers become beacons of compassion, kindness, and empathy. Their unwavering dedication reflects a profound understanding of life's fragility and the sanctity of the human spirit.

These caregivers are the unsung heroes among us, sacrificing their happiness to alleviate the suffering of others. Their calloused and worn hands, shaped by countless hours of caring, possess a gentle touch that heals both seen and unseen wounds. Their embrace offers warmth and understanding, relieving those burdened with pain, fear, and uncertainty.

To all caregivers, an indescribable bond unites you, forged through sacrifice and tested by adversity. Your immeasurable love and unwavering dedication showcase the boundless depths of the human heart. Through your acts, whether grand or humble, you weave the tapestry of human existence, creating a masterpiece of resilience, compassion, and strength.

As I pour my soul onto these pages, I can't help but acknowledge that none of it would have been possible without the enduring love and unwavering support you bestowed upon me, my dearest mother. This dedication is a tribute to you and the profound impact you had on my life and to all caregivers who embody the essence of humanity.

With each word I write, I lay bare the depth of my gratitude, the immensity of my admiration, and the sheer magnitude of my love for you, my mom, and all caregivers who illuminate the world with their immeasurable compassion and kindness.

Mom and Zelda

Mom before the storm

Acknowledgment

I would like to express my deepest gratitude to my mother, the rock of my life, who inspired every word that fills these pages. Your unwavering love and strength have shaped me in ways I could never fully express. I owe the person I am today to your guidance and support.

To my dear daughter, Nicolette, I am endlessly grateful for your unwavering support and understanding during the challenging caregiving moments. Your kindness and love mirrored that of your grandmother, and I am proud to see the compassion you have inherited.

I also extend my heartfelt thanks to all the caregivers who stood by my side and lent their helping hands in caring for my mother. Your compassion and dedication have profoundly impacted our lives, and I am forever grateful for your presence.

And to those who offered support, encouragement, and comfort along the caregiving journey, your presence was felt deeply and appreciated beyond words. Thank you for being pillars of strength during tumultuous times.

This book is a tribute to my mother, Nicolette, all caregivers, and the profound bonds that connect us through love, kindness, and unwavering dedication. Your presence in my life has brought light to the darkest moments, and I am eternally grateful.

karynbanner@gmail.com

About the Author

Karyn resides in Orange County, California, with her daughter Nicolette, two cats, and our pup.

Her passions include advocating for the EndAlzheimers, and the Aids Walk. In her spare time, Karyn enjoys gardening, reading, and the ocean.

CHAPTER ONE

"I AM MY MOTHER'S KEEPER"

In the depths of my heart and soul, I exist as my mother's sight, her voice, and her fleeting memories. I am bound to her, a constant presence in her world as she battles the relentless torment inflicted upon her by her mind. The pain of her condition is profound, a cruel betrayal that knows no mercy.

Once, my mother possessed a brilliant intellect that graced the lecture halls at The University of Michigan, where she held the mantle of an esteemed professor. The subjects she taught were now a mere shadow in the recesses of her mind, eluding her grasp and leaving her stranded in a sea of forgotten knowledge. Yet, I gently whisper her previous forte to her, trying my best to remind her of her past prominence and the respect and admiration she commanded throughout her professional experience.

Her influence reached far beyond the confines of academia. Within the intricate web of the Federal government, my mother once held a position of immense power. She held the highest security clearance one can ever hold in the United States. She had responsibilities on her shoulders and some crucial decisions to make, yet she immersed herself completely in the job she knew she had to do with grace. Those great days of my mother's past are now just distant memories buried beneath the weight of her deteriorating cognition.

A year ago, she stopped listening to books on tape, and her attachments to the stories started to fade away; she could not follow a story. As I sat with her to grasp her experiences, I understood the narratives she once listened to were just a mix of memories and snippets she heard on television. The devotion she once had to comprehend and follow a narrative started to slip through her fingers like grains of sand, leaving her adrift in fragments of recollections and scattered memories.

Some moments break my heart, reminding me of the deep void that has consumed my mother's true essence. I am confronted with the painful truth that she is no longer present, her consciousness fading into the abyss of dementia.

In the sacred realm of kinship, I stand as a daughter bound to my mother by the intricate threads of love and compassion. My journey as her caregiver unfurls with a profound sense of purpose, driven by a spirit that seeks to bring solace to her weary soul.

Within the depths of our shared home, I navigate through the complexities of my mother's diminishing memory, her once vibrant intellect now submerged in the tumultuous waters of dementia. With every passing day, I embrace the role of a guiding light, a source of unwavering support during the storm that ravages her once-pedantic mind.

I tenderly held the pieces of her fading past, some of her cherishing memories, and the struggles she went through. I reignited the embers of her former glory, ensuring her spirit continued to flicker through the encroaching darkness this disease had gotten her into. I forced myself to remind her of her outstanding pursuits and the remarkable impact she had as a professor at a top-notch university. But all of these efforts were a mere challenge due to her illness, which started to take everything away from her.

But it is not merely my duty to preserve her intellectual legacy. No, I am driven by a deeper calling, a selfless devotion to uplift her spirit and alleviate her suffering. In the sacred confines of our home, I embrace the generous ethos of philanthropy, channeling its essence into every moment spent by her side.

I became the embodiment of empathy, witnessing the torment inflicted upon her by her mind and offering my unwavering presence, a comforting balm against the turmoil that engulfed her. With patience and tenderness, I navigated her consciousness, offering solace and reassurance in the face of her mental state.

Together with my daughter, Nicolette, I forge a bond that transcends the traditional roles of caregiver and recipient. We stood as her caregivers with unwavering dedication, united by a belief that one day, my mother would remember everything and live her life the way she did in the past.

I drew strength from the knowledge that my actions, rooted in a philanthropic devotion, held the power to alleviate the burdens that weighed heavily upon my mother's fragile shoulders. As the days passed and the seasons changed, I remained resolute in my commitment to honor her spirit, providing a sanctuary of love and compassion during her heartwarming health condition.

Within the confines of my home, my daughter Nicolette and I have shouldered the immense responsibility of caring for my mother. Four years of unwavering dedication and unconditional love have passed as we strive to provide her with comfort amidst the cruelty of her affliction.

My mother called the coastal sanctuary of Carlsbad, California her home since 2007. Week after week, I dedicated my Saturdays to being by her side, helping her in any way she desired. However, as the insidious grip of Wet Macular Degeneration relentlessly eroded her vision, I knew a difficult decision loomed ahead. With love and concern, I proposed the idea of her moving in with my daughter Nicolette and me in Orange County, hoping to provide the support and care she now needed.

On 09/16/2018, as we meandered through the familiar streets of Carlsbad, I gathered the courage to broach the subject again. With a tender voice, I asked her if she was ready to move in with us.

But she replied,

"No, Zelda would drive me crazy, and I simply want to be alone."

Zelda was our puppy, which ironically became my mother's best friend. As the car rolled on, her voice finally pierced the quiet air, and we realized that she wanted to live alone for now, but the option was always open for her to move in with Nicolette and me. However, the worrying thoughts still flickered through my brain as my mother had been talking about death incessantly for months. She stated that she didn't want to continue her life, but she also solemnly vowed that she would not take matters into her own hands. I knew that her contemplations had shifted elsewhere, and she was consumed by thoughts of mortality, which were now dominating her waking moments. Feelings of emptiness plagued her soul, and her once vibrant intellect was dulled by the limitations imposed by her diminishing senses. I still let her be on her own, worried on my part as I wanted my mother to regain herself in her true personality again.

After almost a year, on 04/05/2019, I received a phone call from my mother, announcing her readiness to move in with us; I felt a surge of urgency pulsating through my veins. With efficiency and determination, I started to organize the packers, movers, and all the details that could make my mother feel comfortable in her new space.

My home, carefully curated to cater to her needs, proved to be the perfect haven for her. A bedroom on the ground floor, blessed with an attached bathroom, removed all the hustles of stepping up the stairs to fulfill her needs. Every area of the house underwent meticulous alterations designed to enhance her safety and support her newfound requirements. Shower bars adorned the bathroom, extending a helping hand in her moments of vulnerability. Soft padding embraced the sharp corners of the sink, mitigating the unforeseen dangers that lurked in the simplest of surroundings. Even in her private sanctuary, we ensured that cable television endowed her bedroom, exclusively tuned to the ever-vital domain of CNN. As a highly esteemed political scientist, she desired to remain abreast of the unfolding currents of our complex world.

A comprehensive shift in the household's landscape ensued as rugs were meticulously removed, exposing a pristine expanse of flooring that facilitated her every step. Sticker buttons were placed on her remote control, coffee maker, microwave, and cell phone as beacons of accessibility, empowering her to use them efficiently as part of her daily routine. These small yet significant modifications were supposed to bestow a profound sense of independence upon her, alleviating the burdens weighing upon her sightless eyes.

I remember when I first laid eyes upon my mother in such a delicate state, my heart sank like a heavy stone descending into the depths of sorrow. Her once strong hands, now weakened and frail, reminded me of the days when she would tightly grasp my small hand, guiding me through bustling markets, treating me to ice cream, and never letting me stray from her loving sight. She was the epitome of a caregiver, devoted to me as if I were the essence of her existence. It was a surreal sight to witness my mother, who had always exuded strength, love, warmth, and beauty, now succumbing to the depths of aging and dementia.

Memories of my childhood and precious moments spent with my mother flooded my mind, spinning like a carousel, filling my heart with an overwhelming wave of pure love and profound respect for the woman who had shaped my world. As I reflected on my mother's unwavering love and care throughout the years, it became clear that it was my turn to reciprocate. It became my sacred duty to offer her the same love, compassion, and unwavering care she had so selflessly bestowed upon me. The memories of her nurturing presence guided me as I embarked upon this journey, demanding resilience, patience, and steadfast commitment. In the corners of my mind, I carefully stored snapshots of moments shared with my mother, like a treasured photograph album filled with snapshots of a life well-lived.

The image of her reading bedtime stories, her soothing voice lulling me to sleep, remained etched in my memory like a gentle lullaby. The aroma of her cooking, lingering in our family kitchen, evoked a sense of security and love. These memories served as a guiding light, reminding me of the depth of her devotion and inspiring me to meet the challenges ahead.

Within the confines of our home, a symphony of meticulous arrangements harmonized, paving the way for my mother's arrival. I anxiously awaited her since it was my turn to make her feel comfortable. Every detail was meticulously considered and impeccably executed, and it stood as a testament to our deep-rooted love and unwavering dedication to her. As the days waned, inching closer to her transformative homecoming, anticipation mingled within Nicolette and me to welcome my mother with our arms wide open.

Mom and Karyn Banner

CHAPTER TWO

"THE MOVE"

On that morning of 05/05/2019, I made my way to Carlsbad with a mix of concern and anticipation. Little did I know that this day would begin a profound chapter in our lives. As I entered her home, I couldn't help but notice the chaos in my mother's kitchen. Time seemed to have halted as if frozen in place, leaving her personal belongings largely untouched. The dishes were neatly stacked on the kitchen rack, gathering a thin layer of dust over the years. Her cherished collection of fine chinaware remained proudly displayed in the showcase, resembling a precious treasure. Every corner of the house vividly painted a picture of her memories, as if preserving them perpetually. The house, in all its stillness, stood as a testament to a life well-lived and cherished.

The gravity of the situation hit me then, and the realization of her deteriorating mind sank in like a heavy weight on my shoulders. It was a stark reminder of the challenges for both of us. But rather than succumbing to despair, a renewed sense of urgency ignited within me. I walked toward the kitchen, carefully examining the items I needed to pack. As I did, thoughts of the things she would want to keep as cherished memories crossed my mind. Simultaneously, I mentally noted what I could take to my home and what things should be stored in my garage for now.

I bid farewell to the familiar with every carefully packed item, knowing that the path ahead was uncertain. Yet, I was determined to embrace the unknown and provide my mother with the comfort she needed. Although anxiety, a constant companion for those living with dementia, gripped her heart, I sought to reassure her.

We headed north, leaving Carlsbad behind. I was confident that I would strengthen our bond no matter how many challenges came my way. For me, this journey was not just a series of events but a tale fueled by love and resilience.

As her daughter, I became a pillar of strength, guiding my mother step by step, reintroducing her memories that were fading slowly because of her memory loss. Deep in my heart, I knew that the journey I had embarked on was of profound significance for me, and I found myself concerned and surrounded with anticipation. I embarked on a journey of profound significance for myself, where I was concerned and surrounded with anticipation and learned that my journey was to serve my mother.

As the movers got to work, tackling the challenging task of packing up her belongings, I delved into the mountains of boxes, carefully storing away the remnants of her familiar life. With each item securely tucked away, I couldn't help but feel the weight of her history resting heavily on my shoulders.

With the moving truck now loaded with all her possessions, my mother and I set off on a journey northward, bidding farewell to Carlsbad. Anxiety, a common companion for those living with dementia, tightly gripped my mother's heart. During those uncertain moments, as her thoughts raced, I sought to reassure her. With sincere words, I painted a picture of our new home, assuring her that it would provide all the comforts she needed. In the meantime, her belongings would find temporary shelter in our garage as she adjusted to this significant change in her life.

Much to my delight, the transition turned out to be smoother than expected. The walls of our new home, once strangers to her, resonated with the echoes of her laughter. Her presence seamlessly intertwined itself into our daily lives. The genuine affection of our beloved dog and two cats enveloped her with a tenderness that she had never experienced with animals during her earlier years. Witnessing the serene joy that she found in their companionship, my daughter Nicolette and I were privileged to witness the transformative power of these four-legged friends.

As May, June, July, and August unfolded, they melded together in a peaceful haze, with only the bright celebration of her birthday in August breaking the tranquility. During those moments, she exhibited pure happiness, her spirit shining with a newfound enthusiasm for life. Despite her faltering memory, she navigated from her bedroom to our shared living room, connecting with my daughters and me on a deeper level. Within the walls of our new sanctuary, she found comfort, and contentment marked her journey of adjusting.

Yet, beneath the calm surface of these uneventful months, a bittersweet reality lingered. We knew deep down that her mind grappled with treacherous waters, eroding the foundation of her memories in silence. And so we cherished these brief moments of connection, intertwining our lives with a delicate thread of love and resilience. Each passing day brought new challenges and opportunities for warmth and affection.

As each day welcomed us with its unique set of trials, I discovered the strength within myself to embrace the role of a caregiver. It was a delicate dance between honoring the woman she once was and accepting the changes that unfolded day by day. I learned to appreciate the beauty in the smallest of moments, the glimmers of recognition that flickered in her eyes when our gazes met or the gentle squeeze of her hand that conveyed her gratitude and love. Though the weight of this responsibility often felt overwhelming, I drew strength from the bond we shared, a bond now tested by the forces of time and circumstance.

In those moments of doubt and weariness, I reminded myself of the vast reservoir of love that resided within me, which had been nurtured by my mother's unwavering presence and affection. In this journey, I came to realize that caring for my mother went beyond the physical tasks of tending to her needs; it was a sacred duty to honor her dignity, preserve her sense of self, and provide comfort during the turbulence of her fading memories.

Through gentle gestures and whispers, I sought to reassure her of the depth of my love, even as her mind became a landscape of scattered fragments, a puzzle missing its essential pieces. The days stretched into weeks, and the weeks melded into months, yet my commitment remained unyielding. I found solace in the enduring power of love when a smile graced her lips, even if only for a fleeting instant. It was a reminder that despite the insidious grip of dementia, the bond between mother and child remained unbreakable.

Within the peaceful haze of the passing months, we provided for her a sanctuary and a steadfast fortress of love and resilience. Our once unfamiliar home now enveloped us with open arms. The walls, once plain, absorbed and reflected the joyful laughter and tender presence of our beloved matriarch.

Hand in hand, we faced the unknown within the walls of our sanctuary. We drew strength from our love, knowing that we could overcome any obstacles together. This journey taught me that even in the face of adversity, beauty can be found. Our story, a testament to resilience, would endure as a legacy of love long after memories had faded.

CHAPTER THREE

"THE BEGINNING OF THE END"

On 01/04/2020, my dear mother faced a multitude of dental troubles. Her bridge, which once served as a sturdy foundation, had completely crumbled, leaving her needing a molar extraction. I took it upon myself to guide her toward the expertise of my remarkable dentist, a master of his craft. With unwavering dedication, he fashioned a custom-made bridge to fit her requirements while simultaneously extracting the infected tooth that had caused her trouble.

To my profound sorrow, my mother refused to embrace this newly crafted dental marvel. She uttered words that echoed with self-assurance, claiming that the bridge was unnecessary and that she did not need it. Little did she know that this would mark the beginning of a profoundly deep decline in her cognitive faculties, diving into a world of confusion and uncertainty.

As the dutiful daughter that I was, it became my unwritten duty to attend to the meticulous care of her hands, ensuring that her fingernails remained trimmed to meticulous precision. A slight scratch, an innocent graze, had the potential to transform into a malicious entity, latching onto her vulnerable flesh and inviting infection. The weight of anxiety emanated through the pores of her skin as I gently administered her bi-weekly manicure, as a ritual born out of love but also one of the necessary things to do for her.

I remember that one seemingly ordinary Tuesday morning when an unforeseen physical anomaly challenged the routine. As I began to work my nurturing hands upon her weathered fingers, I noticed a slight constriction in her right middle finger, causing a delicate ripple to extend towards her adjacent ring finger. Concerned and sensing the gravity of the situation, we visited her physician's office, never suspecting the difficult journey that lay before us.

What was intended to be a 15-minute appointment stretched into a three-hour long appointment. Within the confines of that sterile chamber, our hope crumbled like an ancient stone, crushed beneath the weight of her blindness and her newfound unsteadiness. My mother reluctantly embraced the confines of a wheelchair; the whims of an unyielding affliction stole her freedom.

In these difficult moments, the veil of darkness threatened to shroud her entire being; philosophical musings flickered and danced among the shadows. Life appeared as a picture framed with triumph and tragedy. Each passing second revealed the fragility of my mother's existence, challenging the essence of her life. During these difficult times, we found ourselves compelled to redefine our purpose and seek solace and strength when surrounded by uncalled chaos.

I kept on walking on the difficult path of love and loss ahead of me, where I had no other choice but to keep walking forward, embracing the unknown with determination. I held hope, protecting my heart and soul with resilience and endurance. I knew God was testing me because, in the crucible of adversity, the essence of the human spirit was revealed; I made sense of this for a long while. I found my true spirit to be with my mother, never leaving by her side. I was determined to take care of my mother, and I decided to hold her hand through every phase of life.

Since it was a long appointment with the physician, we were told multiple conditions my mother had. The physician unveiled another awful diagnosis, labeling her condition as "dementia clenched fist," which prompted a referral to a hand specialist. The specialist explained that surgery was an option, but unfortunately, it was not feasible due to the progression of her dementia. Instead, they suggested exploring the avenue of physical therapy. Our physical therapy journey commenced on 01/21/2020, with a four-hour round trip, including a mere half-hour of therapy.

Upon each physical therapy visit, the rituals began with applying a gentle heating pad to her hand, aiming to alleviate the stiffness within her joints. However, during our inaugural session, she insisted that the heating pad was not functioning despite my touch confirming its warmth. It was at that moment when I realized she had lost the ability to effectively communicate pain and sensations. Her decline was accelerating rapidly, and it was heartbreaking for us to see her in this condition.

Nevertheless, I emphatically reassured her that her physical therapist was exceptional and the heating pad was functioning as intended. To aid her struggle against her clenched fist, the physical therapist ingeniously crafted a custom hand brace, with the intention for my mother to wear it consistently; it was to maintain an open hand posture for her. However, the progress achieved during physical therapy proved to be futile as my mother, throughout the night, persistently removed the brace, effectively erasing any positive impact made. It became obvious that our battle was one with diminishing odds of victory.

During our last visit to the physical therapist in late June 2020, something unexpected happened that affected our plans. My mother suddenly had to use the restroom and couldn't make it in time, resulting in an unfortunate accident that soiled her clothes. It was a public place, and I found myself responsible for cleaning up the mess, a duty I never expected to take. This incident marked the beginning of a challenging situation—her incontinence—that required quick action to preserve her dignity.

To ease the distress caused by these unforeseen circumstances, I suggested getting adult pull-ups—practical and compassionate garments that would provide some insurance against similar instances. Thankfully, my mother agreed, realizing the need for such support. On 5/5/2020, mom sat on the ottoman in the living room, unaware of the dangers awaiting her. It was probably a lapse in judgment that led to a distressing fall onto the hard floor; she crashed straight into the bookcase. Nicolette helped me pick mom up, for which I was extremely grateful. Thankfully, my mother didn't suffer any injuries that day, providing a momentary break from the ongoing challenges surrounding her.

From her fall that day, a demanding routine took shape, and it became a daily ritual that tested our patience and resilience in handling such situations. Accidents in her pull-ups became regular, an unwelcome companion that followed her every step. Something as simple as showering turned into a bittersweet task performed almost daily, reminding us of life's fragility.

Deep contemplations emerged from the necessary routines in those moments of personal care. Life, we realized, was unpredictable, defying our desire for stability. The human experience, mysterious and multifaceted, revealed both vulnerabilities and strengths. Between the turbulent waves of our shared journey, our humanity stood bare—a testament to the unyielding spirit required to navigate such trials.

One truth remained constant throughout the challenges we faced—the unbreakable bond between a mother and child. As I witnessed her struggles, a profound sense of empathy surged through me, fueling a fierce determination to protect her dignity and shield her from the blows that she had to deal with. It was a sacred obligation out of love and unwavering support for my mother.

The days became difficult with time, marked by setbacks and obstacles; a flicker of hope persisted during the darkness. Despite the weight of her deteriorating condition, love remained constant—a guiding light illuminating our path. Although the road ahead appeared uncertain and scary, our strong bond served as a compass, leading us through the unknown depths of her incontinence.

In this delicate emotion filled with resilience, love emerged as the anchor preventing us from being overwhelmed by the storms of hardships. Hence, each day was met with utmost determination, cherishing moments, and finding solace in our resilient spirits.

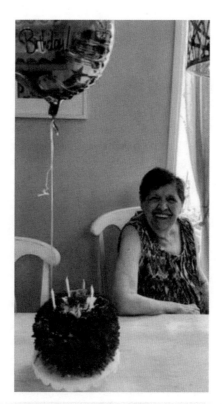

Mom's 86th Birthday

CHAPTER FOUR

"HALLUCINATIONS"

During each doctor's appointment, my mom was asked how she felt, and I was expected to respond on her behalf, as those were answers she could no longer convey. It was always an emotional task, trying to accurately relay her experiences and emotions without losing sight of my own. Today, we also had a haircut appointment, a seemingly routine task that took on a new significance now that all medical and ancillary services were provided in-house.

On 7/25/2020, my mom started speaking in a whisper-like voice, which was when her hallucinations started. When I asked her why she was whispering, she said she didn't know why. On 9/30/2020, she mentioned that she'd like to cook for our neighbor Travis, and then later that day, she asked if he liked the meal. Just a day ago, mom's television didn't "shut off" randomly like it does every day, five times a day. Mom got irritated as she fiddled with the remote, and everything became discombobulated.

On the crisp autumn day of 9/04/2020, a chilling shift swept through our lives like a whisper of foreboding wind. My beloved mother, once vibrant and full of life, began to fade before our eyes. She took solace in smaller portions, her appetite waning like the last light of a dying flame. Sleep enveloped her like a heavy quilt, pulling her deeper into its embrace each day.

But it wasn't just her physical being that transformed; her essence, her very being, seemed to unravel. Memories, once sharp as a freshly honed blade, now slipped through her grasp like grains of sand through her fingers. Her emotions became a tumultuous sea, tossing between waves of laughter, tears, kindness, and cruelty, leaving us stranded on the shores of uncertainty.

In moments of lucidity, her eyes, once filled with warmth and recognition, gazed into the void with vacant stares, as if searching for a beacon in the fog of her mind. She had confused faces, mistaking my daughter Nic for myself and blurring the lines between reality and illusion.

Yet amidst this chaos, she remained steadfast in her insistence that all was well, that she had battled and overcome the invisible specter of COVID-19, a phantom that never haunted our home. Oh, how desperately she clung to this facade, this fragile veil of normalcy, even as the truth slipped further from her grasp with each passing day.

On 9/13/2020, around 1:30 PM, I asked mom if she'd eaten some cookies instead of lunch since she wasn't hungry. She denied having any cookies, leaving me puzzled. Today, after a whole week, we finally convinced her to shower. Alzheimer's patients dread showering, making it a tough task. It felt like a small win in our ongoing battle against the disease.

On the gentle breeze of 9/16/2020, a friendly doctor visited our home, a weekly treat for my mom, who found traveling a bit tough those days. The doctor gave mom a flu shot today. But like a whisper in the wind, the whole visit slipped from mom's memory, except for the little ache in her arm. So, I softly reminded her about the shot she got, hoping to bring back a glimpse of that fleeting moment.

Yet, as swiftly as the physician's visit had come, it slipped from mom's grasp like sand through an hourglass. All but a fleeting memory remained, captured in the ache of her arm where the needle had pierced. With tenderness, I gently reminded her of the doctor's visit and the purpose behind the sting in her flesh, a reminder of the fleeting nature of time and memory in the dance of life.

On 9/18/2020, a mobile phlebotomist arrived for a blood draw and urinalysis. Unfortunately, only the blood draw went smoothly, leaving a sense of disappointment lingering in the air.

Then, on 9/22/2020, a poignant moment unfolded in our kitchen. Nic, with tender care, prepared a brisket, hoping to bring comfort to our home. But amidst the aroma of cooking meat, tragedy struck as her grandma, in her declining state, mistook the oven for a serving dish, attempting to carve a slice before it was ready. Nic's words, filled with concern, echoed through the room, warning against consuming the raw meat. It was a moment that captured the bittersweet essence of our journey, reminding us of the fragility of life and the challenges we face together.

Then, on 10/17/2020, a poignant moment unfolded in the quiet of our kitchen. Mom emerged, greeting the morning as if it were anew, unaware of the passage of time. With gentle reassurance, we reminded her of the breakfast she had already enjoyed, highlighting the cruel grasp dementia holds over her sense of time, leaving her adrift in a sea of confusion.

On 10/25/2020, another tender interaction unfolded as Nic shared news of a homemade squash soup. Mom lost in the labyrinth of her memories, mistook it for her own creation. In these moments, we've learned the art of "therapeutic fibs," embracing gentle truths to soothe a troubled mind, for there is no reasoning with the relentless grip of dementia.

On 11/1/2020, a heartwarming routine began as my eldest daughter, Gabrielle, dedicated her Sundays to showering her grandmother. Despite the fog of dementia clouding grandma's mind, Gabrielle's presence provided a sense of comfort and familiarity, even if recognition remained elusive for all of us.

Christmas Day, 12/25/2020, was a delightful day. Our traditional Christmas meal presents, which mom enjoyed immensely. My daughters, mom, and I had a wonderful Christmas!

On 1/21/2021, a physician's visit marked a sobering reality check. Mom's once vibrant spirit was now confined to a bed, her body betraying her with each passing day. The doctor's concern over her deteriorating physical health mirrored our fears. Mom's mind, once sharp, now resembled that of a young child, lost in a world of sensory overload and confusion. With each appointment, the weight of responsibility rested heavily on my shoulders as I became her voice in a world she struggled to navigate. The doctor was concerned about the poor circulation of her legs and feet. It was also noted that her time for remembering recent events has dwindled to 30 minutes. Mom was now akin to that of a 4-year-old child. She had begun picking her ears, nose, and teeth, then eating whatever came out. Mom was no longer able to differentiate between pain and warmth. She was so extremely anxious and overwhelmed, and she is experiencing sensory overload. Mom was asked how she felt about each doctor's appointment and then looked at me to respond.

On 2/12/2021, amidst the backdrop of our in-house medical and ancillary services, a bittersweet event unfolded: haircut day. Despite protests of fatigue and stomach discomfort, mom reluctantly acquiesced. However, her appetite betrayed her, indulging solely in chocolate-covered strawberries and cheesecake, a testament to the cravings common among dementia patients. We tread carefully, avoiding fried foods to avert bathroom mishaps. It became apparent that mom only liked sweets and carbs, which is very common with dementia patients.

6/10/2021 cast a shadow over our home, marked by numerous bathroom accidents and showers. Mom, refusing nourishment, drove me to tears as I mourned the loss of her once-brilliant mind. Some days weighed heavier than others, testing our resilience and the strength of our bond. On one such day, multiple bathroom accidents demanded immediate attention. Showers became necessary, an intricate dance of water and soap to cleanse away the mess and the remnants of frustration. While attending to her physical needs, I couldn't help but ache inside for the brilliant mind slipping away, leaving behind a hollow emptiness. The person I once shared laughter and secrets with was drifting further away, and the grief welled up within me, crashing against the barricades I had tried so hard to fortify.

Yet, amidst the turmoil, a glimmer of relief emerged on 6/21/2021, with the arrival of bathers to assist mom's hygiene routine. They came every Monday, Wednesday, and Friday. Their thrice-weekly visits and Gabrielle's Sunday showers aimed to combat infections rampant among dementia patients. Special care was given to mom's right hand, a roll of gauze serving as a barrier against self-inflicted harm.

As the challenges multiplied, so did our attempts to find solace in moments of respite. I had once entertained the idea of setting up a CD player or providing books on tape, offering a window into worlds she could no longer physically see. But even that gentle sanctuary had slipped through our fingers. Mom could no longer follow a story on tape, her once-attentive mind unraveling narrative threads. Instead, the television became her lifeline, and the familiar voices on CNN filled her days. The volume was always set at 26, a point of stability in a world spinning out of control.

On 7/1/2021, the day was tinged for my mom with memories of her Dad as she yearned for his presence, seeking solace in the distant remnants of their bond. It became evident that Nic was correct; mom could no longer differentiate whether she was hungry. From then on, we had to inform her of meal times and assist her with eating. Our approach shifted to using bowls and spoons instead of forks or plates.

By 7/9/2021, mom's appetite dwindled further, limited to a mere piece of toast. Desperate measures ensued as we stocked her bedside table with snacks (chips and candies) in hopes of coaxing nourishment.

From 7/12/2021, Nicolette was responsible for waking my mother up at 11:00 am. The ritual involved administering her medications, carefully guiding her to the bathroom, changing her clothes, and eventually returning her to the comfort of her bed. Despite preparing breakfast, her eating patterns became unpredictable, with some days when she barely touched her meal.

There was a glimmer of hope during a particular doctor's appointment on 7/13/2021. When I returned home at 4 pm, with Nicolette still at home, she surprised us all by showing an appetite. She managed to devour a chicken thigh and a biscuit. Remarkably, as I took away her plate, it seemed like she craved something else. I gently asked if she needed anything, and with a longing look, she replied, "Something to eat." Though I reminded her she had just eaten, I couldn't resist appeasing her with a serving of ice cream. The joy on her face was immeasurable as she eagerly savored each spoonful.

In a heartfelt message to uncle Jerry on 7/20/2021, amidst the week's turmoil, a rare moment of clarity surfaced as my mother expressed genuine appreciation for her brother. She also talked to him, but I didn't know whether uncle Jerry was aware of her condition.

On the same day, I messaged my mom's brother, uncle Jerry, to inform him that I had my mom talk to Aunt Thelma and then suggested to her, "How about I get your brother on the phone?" This week has been particularly challenging with my mother's condition, but tonight, there was a brief moment of clarity. I told my uncle that I truly appreciate him and think he is kind and good. My mom said, "I always feel better after talking to my brother." Witnessing these fleeting moments of clarity is incredibly difficult for the caregiver. Witnessing such fleeting moments of clarity served as a poignant reminder of the woman she once was, juxtaposed against the painful reality of her decline.

On 8/12/2021, when I went to the park that night, my mom was on the phone with her brother, uncle Jerry. Nic came home, and mom asked her who her mother was. Nic replied, "Karyn." Then mom asked Nic, "Then that makes you who?" It was a surreal experience, as her brain seemed to be tormenting her.

On 8/17/2021, my mother slept in late until 12:30. She seemed exhausted and worn out. Lunch was at 4, dinner at 8:45 pm. We opted for a quick meal, as she knew it was late, having beef and potatoes instead of pizza or lasagna. As I left her room, she said, "I know it's past your bedtime; I won't need anything else." I reassured her it wasn't my bedtime, but it was too late for steak and potatoes, so I made her a hearty sandwich.

On 8/18/2021, it was challenging to care for my mother every day, given her condition. Dementia patients could often be hostile or aggressive. Surprisingly, my mom was only slightly unpleasant. She showed extreme kindness, gentleness, and gratitude for our care as we progressed. We were extremely lucky there was never any aggression or hostility.

On 10/3/2021, after returning from the park, I asked mom if she was ready for dinner, and she said, "Not yet." She inquired about Nic, mentioning she hadn't seen her in days. I found Nic upstairs and confirmed she had already eaten.

On 10/10/2021, I felt the weight of sadness and depression as my mother no longer recognized me or my daughters. Watching my daughter, Nicolette, witness this unfolding situation was a heartbreaking experience for all of us. It was a heartbreaking reality to witness unfold, and it filled me with deep sorrow. Nicolette felt the weight of this situation, and her sadness mirrored mine.

On 10/12/2021, during a conversation with Kim, the daughter of my mom's oldest and dearest friend, I inquired about her mom's well-being. Kim sadly shared that her mother was not doing well and was under hospice care, heavily reliant on morphine. Recurring urinary tract infections had taken a toll on her, necessitating the use of a catheter. Kim then asked about my mom. We called her, and Bette's speech was rambling, likely a side effect of the morphine.

It was a poignant moment as these longtime friends, who knew each other intimately, exchanged affectionate words like "sweetheart" and expressed their love. It felt like a bittersweet goodbye, tinged with the recognition of the inevitable.

It was 10/23/2021, and it had been three days since mom wasn't feeling well.   Her health continued to deteriorate. She expressed feelings of weakness, although she did not have a fever. Her appetite had diminished, and she was barely eating and drinking. The exhaustion had taken its toll on her. Meanwhile, Nicolette was away in Palm Springs, seeking a much-needed break from the emotional weight of the situation.

As the days passed, the heaviness in my heart remained, knowing that my mom's condition was declining. The uncertainties and challenges of this journey weighed upon me, and I longed for moments of respite and strength to carry me through.

CHAPTER FIVE

"CONFLICTING EMOTIONS — FURTHER DECLINE"

On 10/26/2021, mom's oldest and best friend passed away, and I received a call from her daughter Kim informing me of the sad news. It was a sad moment, knowing that our moms had recently spoken. Despite the burial being live-streamed, I chose not to share it with mom as she quickly forgot about the death after I told her.

On 11/10/2021, a worrisome incident occurred when Nicolette went to take the dog out and discovered grandma asleep on the bathroom floor. Nic's eyes showed evident fear as they wondered if mom had fallen while making her way to the bathroom, visibly shaking. I carefully checked her for injuries but thankfully found none. I ordered an alarm pad for my mother's bed and kept the monitor in my room to ensure her safety. It's truly heart-wrenching to witness these events unfold, and I'm also deeply concerned about its impact on Nicolette.

Seeking some respite, on 11/12/2021, I decided to hire a part-time caregiver to assist us. Initially, mom exhibited hostility towards her, adding to the emotional weight of the situation. But over the next year and a half, they developed a deep connection that brought solace amidst the challenges. They affectionately referred to each other as "good girls."

However, there were still moments of struggle, such as mom adamantly resisting a shower and claiming she had already taken on the day before. Later that day, she resisted a shower again and said she had taken one the previous day! She told Nic, " Just put me in a home." Nic responded, "A home will be far stricter!" Our caregiver got her to shower and eat lunch in the living room! She was wonderful! It was a heartening sight to witness our caregiver skillfully navigate these challenges, successfully convincing mom to shower and adapt to having her lunch in the living room.

On 12/1/2021, the morning began with mom in a foul mood. When Gabrielle came over, mom looked at her as if she didn't recognize her. Soon after, mom had a massive diarrhea incident in her bathroom, which Gabrielle graciously cleaned up.

On 12/9/2021, Gabrielle paid another visit today. During our time together, my mother suggested that we all go visit Shirley, my sister-in-law, who resides in a dementia home. I gently reminded her that Shirley was actually in Vermont, but I promised to give her a call. As my mother began recounting stories from the house I grew up in, she once again mistook Gabrielle for me. Mom also mentioned her dear friend Bette. Little did she know, a heavy burden lay upon me— an unbearable task of imparting the heart-wrenching news, again. Bette had passed away. Sorrow blanketed the room as I gently shared the tragic truth. In response, she sought solace, immediately asking the painful question: When did it happen? With trembling words, I explained it had been approximately four weeks ago. Mom's reaction was simply indifferent.

The weight of those crushing words lingered in the air, permeating my being with profound sadness. A torrent of emotions overwhelmed me, yet amidst this emotional turmoil, the day unfolded with a semblance of normalcy.

It was 12/13/2021, and the relentless battle with explosive diarrhea continued on that day; I witnessed the constant struggle imposed upon my mother, regardless of what she consumed. The never-ending cleaning of her bathroom became a grim routine. The overwhelming nature of it all threatened to engulf me, pushing me to the edge of my patience. All that remained was a fragile semblance of control, even if it meant constantly replacing toilet seats to reclaim some modicum of stability. But in those moments of frustration, I summoned the strength to remind myself that my mother's suffering far outweighed any inconvenience or personal frustration I might experience.

On 12/14/2021, the camera in my mother's room confirmed that she slept through the night. Frequently, I checked the camera's footage for any changes or movement. The footage showed that she would usually be asleep or sitting up, staring off into the distance. It saddened me to observe this.

The days marched on, and on 12/17/2021, I undertook bathing my beloved mother. My sanity found solace in the presence of a humble shower chair—a faithful companion in the arduous ordeal. A toilet seat riser with sturdy handles adorned the bathroom to offer her a greater sense of security. After her shower, she was trying to put on the old pull-up, a used one. I told her she uses a new one each time. These tender moments served as a poignant reminder of the immense responsibility I carried upon my shoulders.

On 12/25/2021, Christmas came and went, and I was happy to celebrate it with my mom and daughters by my side. The rituals unfolded, mundane yet poignant.

On New Year's Eve of 2022, reflections on how my life had come to a standstill during my mother's final days lingered in my mind. She had led an exceptional and successful career path. The night evoked memories of my long-standing tradition of driving to the beach at midnight, sitting alone in the sand, and watching fireworks, a practice I had neglected for the past three years.

Being there brought to mind the need to ensure my mother's safety, as even a short walk to the garage alone posed risks due to the presence of a lurking mountain lion. These responsibilities served as a reminder of my current priorities.

Despite the solemn undertones, the evening progressed with a pleasant charcuterie spread and a bottle of cabernet that added a touch of warmth to the atmosphere.

On 1/7/2022, another round of World War 3 commenced with the challenge of showering. I look forward to facing this battle once more on Monday. I thank our caregiver for her unwavering patience and strength during these trying times.

On 1/8/2022, the day was marked by a series of challenges. She exhibited unpleasant behavior towards our caregiver, instructing her to leave and expressing frustration. A significant argument ensued over the necessity of a shower, the first one in four days. The aftermath of such incidents poses the greatest challenge for the caregiver, as they often do not remember the events while we carry the weight of these difficult interactions.

It became completely evident on 1/12/2022 that mom's short-term memories had completely vanished, leaving her grasping at moments from the distant past that are still vivid in her mind. I found myself pondering what her final memory might be as she navigates through this challenging phase of memory loss.

On 1/13/2022, a concerning episode unfolded as mom recounted a vivid memory to Nic. She shared that she had heard something near the front door the previous night, prompting her to open the door, only to find a mountain lion outside the house. This incident may have stemmed from memories of her time living in Irvine, per my mom's recollections. Despite this event, the security camera footage confirmed that she had not left her bed overnight. Mom expressed anxiety about the situation, urging me to inform all the neighbors. The hallucinations mom experienced seemed to be increasing in frequency, signaling a troubling development.

On 1/14/2022, I informed mom that it was my youngest brother's birthday and suggested we call him. During the conversation, mom repeatedly referred to him as her baby, conveying a sense of finality in her words. This sentiment echoed in her interactions with my eldest brother when she asked him to visit the previous week. Observations from my brother suggested that mom's health may be declining, a realization that we have slowly come to accept.

On 1/16/2022, a phone call between my mother and my third brother took an unexpected turn. As they conversed casually about the weather, my mother innocently stated, "It's 6 degrees here." Perplexed, my brother questioned her location, to which she matter-of-factly replied, "Colorado."

I promptly entered her room, gently informing her we were, in fact, in California, accompanied by Nicolette, where the weather boasted a delightful 70 degrees. It was a moment of gentle correction, a reminder of the confusion that had trapped her mind.

It was the same day I kept thinking about my mother. Tears silently flowed, with no dreams to unveil the source of my pain. My heart shattered into fragments, engulfed by an overwhelming ache. Desperate, I redirected my focus to my mother, recognizing the immense fear that gripped her fragile existence. I reassured myself, vowing to handle this dire situation with unwavering strength.

On 01/17/2022, I entered her bedroom and cautiously uttered, "I want to ask you a question."

In response, she shared her persistent thoughts, a desire buried deep within her. The words spilled forth, haphazardly weaving tales of her unconventional past, where women seldom made the first move in their marriages. Yet, she defied societal norms in her unyielding yearning for a daughter. The realization dawned upon me through her disjointed narratives—the question I posed might elude her fragile grasp. Her mind wandered, lost in a labyrinth of tangents. Regret gnawed at me as I had waited too long, allowing time to erode her understanding. However, my inherent nature compelled me to unveil the truth. Amidst the chaos of her scattered thoughts, I revealed the depth of my inquiry. Did she, perchance, long for a girl? The answer eluded her fragmented consciousness, yet it did not lose the significance of her influence on me. In that tender moment, I acknowledged her as my guiding light, a beacon of independence and strength, and my unwavering hero.

With the arrival of 1/24/2022, my mother's slumber ceased at 8:45 am, undisturbed by the night. A disquietude loomed, leaving her in a state of irritability and fatigue. She declared her desire to keep our caregiver at a distance, noting her sensitivity. Weariness plagued her throughout the day, manifesting in a diminished appetite during dinner.

2/10/2022 etched itself into the timeline as a day of tribulations. Three incidents of diarrhea demanded my attention, intensifying the laborious task of cleaning, which inevitably led to three showers. My mother's dietary preferences remained enigmatic, as she oscillated between liking a particular food one day and scorning it the next. Chaos permeated her existence, devoid of any discernible pattern or reason.

CHAPTER SIX

"NAVIGATING DIFFICULT DAYS AND NEW CHALLENGES"

On 2/12/2022, I woke mom up at 1:00 p.m. for breakfast, followed by lunch at 4:30 p.m. Later in the day, Gabrielle visited to assist with showering.

On 2/21/2022, I found myself reminiscing, searching for those fragments of time that had stood still. As we age, we are naturally inclined to seek familiarity, comfort, and roots. Little did I know that the events would shape the next chapter of our lives.

It was the day mom's aunt passed away. The news hit us hard, especially mom, as they had shared an incredibly close bond. However, there was something I had to withhold from her. The funeral was going to be held online, and I knew deep down that mom wouldn't be able to comprehend or participate in such an arrangement.

Fast forward to 3/1/2022, mom's restless nights had become a norm. She was up at 11:00 pm, then 12:30 am, 1 am, 2 am, and 3 am. As part of my daily routine, I would check the video footage from the previous night in her room before heading downstairs. It was a bittersweet ritual, a reminder of time slipping away.

3/7/2022 arrived, and the weight of the situation could no longer be ignored. Mom was growing weaker by the day, and she began relying on her whisper voice once again. It was heartbreaking to witness her struggle, to see her dignity fade as illness took its toll.

Days turned into weeks, and on 3/20/2022, tragedy struck yet again. My amazing sister-in-law lost her battle with early-onset Alzheimer's, FTD. She was an angel, a beautiful soul forever etched in our hearts. Her spirit inspired me, pushing me to achieve more and embrace kindness. The pain my brother felt was immeasurable, knowing he had lost a lifetime of love and companionship.

3/22/2022 was a test of strength. I shielded mom from calling my brother until Monday, as I knew her mental state was fragile, as well as his. But when she finally spoke with him, confusion settled in. She began retelling a story about "her daughter-in-law" being her daughter among the five kids. My brother erupted with anger, unable to bear witness to mom's fading memory. He understood the grief and the magnitude of the loss more than anyone else. He was grieving a paramount loss. Rest in peace, dear sister-in-law, and your love will forever be cherished.

Two days later, on 3/26/2022, mom's deteriorating condition was evident. She seemed unwell. When I asked if anything hurt, her response shattered my heart. "I feel like nothing," she whispered. It became clear that mom was disassociating from everything, fading away into a realm beyond our reach.

As the month drew to a close on 3/28/2022, I sat beside mom, offering her some solace. I suggested playing Vivaldi, but she declined, stating that she needed to stay current with world events. It struck me—she had once been a decision-maker, someone who held the power to shape the world. Now, she clung to those fragments of memory, craving a connection to the present.

And thus, our story continues, intertwined with emotions, drama, and the relentless passage of time.

4/4/2022 arrived, and the sight of my mother startled me. She looked like a ghost, her skin ashen, her eyes distant and empty. Her voice was reduced to a whisper, a fragile thread holding onto life. I couldn't help but wonder if she was waiting for something, some sign that would release her from her suffering.

4/21/2022 brought tears to mom's eyes as she expressed her deep sadness. She missed her father immensely, reminiscing about the love he had showered upon her. Memories of her sister also surfaced, recalling when she used to call her "Nanny" as a child, unable to pronounce "Nancy." It was difficult to witness the toll this disease took on her, drawing parallels between the destructive behaviors of addiction and the relentless grip of dementia. Each day presented unexpected challenges, leaving caregivers blindsided while the patients themselves were oblivious to it all. It was an experience few could comprehend without living through it.

5/1/2022 held a glimmer of remembrance. Nic, my daughter, reminded mom that it was my birthday. We had learned that it was best to inform mom about important events a few minutes before they happened. It was a tender moment, a temporary respite from the relentless progression of her illness.

5/5/2022 brought a barrage of bodily discomfort. Mom experienced bouts of poop, vomit, and diarrhea throughout the day, seemingly without any specific cause. The doctor recommended medications like Imodium and Pepto Bismol to provide some relief. Meanwhile, mom slept through most of the day and night, seeking solace in her slumber.

5/16/2022 greeted me with a sense of despair. I found myself waking up early with a heavy heart and a sense of helplessness. It seemed as if my life had been put on hold, overshadowed by the excruciating decline of my beloved mother. I yearned for guidance, a mentor who could provide comfort and direction. Despite being a grown woman, I felt lost, like a child adrift in a vast sea of uncertainty.

The weight of the situation intensified with each passing day. The light that once filled my mother's eyes was gradually fading, and I couldn't help but confront the painful reality that lay ahead.

On 5/31/2022, Gabrielle arrived to shower mom, but tiredness and weakness prevented her from completing the task. This was a stark reminder that showering was an absolute necessity tomorrow. The urgency in my thoughts reflected the overwhelming responsibilities and challenges of caregiving.

As May drew to a close and June rolled in on 6/20/2022, I longed for moments of happiness. It seemed that leaving the confines of our house was the only time I could truly find solace. The weight of caregiving took its toll both on Nicolette and me as we watched my mom slip further away. During this heart-wrenching journey, I was grateful to have Nicolette by my side, serving as a source of strength and support. 6/24/2022 presented an opportunity to connect with memories of joy. I informed mom that it was her third son's birthday, suggesting we make a video call. The conversation was confusing, yet mom wished him a happy birthday. It was a bittersweet moment, marked by the realization that her grasp on reality was fading.

On 6/25/2022, I discovered mom on the floor when I went to take the pup out at 5:00 pm. She mentioned that she had slid off the bed and had been there for a while, choosing not to press her alert button to avoid disturbing me while I was on the sofa. Despite no apparent injuries, my heart raced with worry while she laughed it off, claiming it was not a significant event. The isolating nature of this disease weighed heavily on me, prompting a need to seek support and talk to someone soon.

On 6/26/2022, I was greeted with the familiar theme of waiting. I attempted to wake my mother at 11:30 am for breakfast, but she resisted, citing fatigue and no reason to rise. Perhaps the previous day's fall had left her disoriented. Hours passed, and the isolation settled in as I waited for her to awaken. The struggles of isolation were compounded by the constant battle against ants and the need to be patient when she dropped food unknowingly. The weight of my responsibilities started to take a toll on my mental well-being. Finally, at 2:00 pm, I woke her, and she reluctantly ate breakfast. Confusion marred her words, and she expressed weakness and soreness. Being confined within the house for an entire day amplified the feeling of being an outsider, with only brief moments to step outside with the puppy. The walls closed in as the isolation took its toll on both me and my mother.

CHAPTER SEVEN

"LIFE IN TRANSITION"

On 7/04/2022, a warm and delightful day, I savored a mouthwatering feast of succulent ribs, golden corn on the cob, and creamy mashed potatoes. The flavors danced on my taste buds as the summer sun embraced us. Sitting across from me, my dear mother relished every bite, her eyes sparkling with pure joy. It was a moment of pure bliss.

Fast forward to 7/15/2022, I returned home after visiting my brother in Vermont. Fatigue clung to my bones as I wearily stepped through the front door. Desiring nothing more than a comforting presence, I sought solace in my mother's company. Her expression softened when I mentioned my journey to Vermont, and she inquired about my brother's well-being. With a heavy heart, I again shared the news of Shirley's passing. Her face contorted with disbelief and sorrow as the words left my lips. Memories of her recent trip to Burlington flooded her thoughts, emphasizing the cruel reality of this insidious disease that robs us of our loved ones. The weight of that moment lingered in the air, a poignant reminder of life's fragility. Mom had not been to Burlington in many years.

Days turned into weeks, and the passage of time brought further heartache. Faint and fragile, my mother's voice trembled as she whispered her words, a stark contrast to her once vibrant self. As I led our furry companion outside one evening, she mustered the strength to inquire about the hour. "Is it or pm?" she asked, her voice choked with uncertainty. A wave of sadness washed over me, witnessing her clarity and awareness gradually fade.

On 7/30/2022, the moments of confusion and distress continued to unfold, leaving us both bewildered and helpless. One afternoon, after my mother had her midday meal at 12:30, I embarked on a futile mission to locate a mysterious "bad smell" that plagued her senses. I scoured her surroundings for thirty minutes, desperate to put her mind at ease. Alas, my efforts were in vain, for there was nothing amiss. The trashcan remained devoid of soiled diapers, her hygiene was impeccable, and the kitty litter was pristine as always. Perhaps I was chasing shadows, searching for answers that were never meant to be found.

On 7/31/2022, as the evening drew near, I collected the remnants of my mother's 8:45 dinner from her room. She claimed to have discovered an ant lurking within her meal in a perplexing twist. I assured her that this was not the case, reminding her minutes before to keep her cupcake away from her room to prevent the invasion of unwanted pests. Despite my fervent efforts to maintain a clean and ant-free environment, her diminishing sight caused her to drop morsels of food onto the floor. Still, she insisted that her dinner bore witness to many ants, a figment of her failing perception.

But amidst the trials and tribulations, moments of unforeseen enchantment unfolded. On a whimsical evening of 8/7/2022, we celebrated Nic's birthday with an intimate dinner accompanied by delectable cupcakes. Gabrielle's boyfriend joined us, and a warm and charming presence added to the festivities. It was then that my mother, in her fleeting clarity, regaled us with tales of her half-brothers and half-sisters. Unbeknownst to us, her father had another family, and she shared these anecdotes with a twinkle in her eye. Despite the bittersweet knowledge that her hallucinations were accelerating, this evening provided a glimpse of respite from the shadows that haunted us.

Unbeknownst to us, her father had created another life, and the intricacies of her newfound family tree unfolded with each chapter she shared. The room was captivated, hanging onto her words like fragile pieces of a fading legacy. But behind the enchantment of that evening, the relentless progression of her hallucinations loomed like an approaching storm. The grip of this relentless disease tightened with each passing day like a relentless adversary taunting our resilience. The boundaries between truth and illusion were blurred, leaving us both entangled in a world where reality shifted like a mirage. Yet, amidst the chaos and the ghosts that haunted us, we forged deep connections and found strength in our vulnerability.

Every moment spent on my mother's side became a testament to the depths of unconditional love. We navigated the treacherous terrain of memory loss and fragmented moments, holding each other's hands tightly as we traversed the winding path of this unforgiving journey. As the summer days waned and the sun descended, we clung to each sliver of fleeting clarity, knowing that the distance between us widened with every breath. But through the tears and the ache in our hearts, we vowed to cherish the moments of connection, the whispers of a shared past that still flickered in the depths of her consciousness.

And so, we braced ourselves for the tumultuous storm ahead, armed with love and resilience, as we faced the uncharted territory of a tomorrow filled with uncertainty. In the face of adversity, we found solace in the simple yet profound moments that stitched together the tapestry of her life. We prepared ourselves for the battles yet to come, united in our commitment to navigate this unrelenting journey hand in hand, forever bound by the unbreakable ties of kinship and devotion.

On 8/8/2022, a heavy weight settled upon our hearts as even our exceptional caregiver, Siobhan, expressed concern. "She's weaker, tired," she mentioned, her voice laced with apprehension and sadness. The sight of our dear one withering away before our eyes is excruciating to bear. Fear grips me tightly, its icy fingers constricting my chest, for I cannot fathom a world without her. Is it because I will no longer be identified as "Karyn, the caregiver?" That realization, as painful as it is, gnaws at the corners of my mind. Yet, beneath her once vibrant eyes, darkened bags have taken residence. Approximately a week ago, they emerged, accompanied by a haunting fatigue she could no longer escape. She could only faintly whisper, "I'm so tired."

On 8/11/2022, Nic ventured off to Yosemite in the company of a friend, and anticipation mingled with fond memories of past celebrations. The day grew tired, and Nic returned home as twilight painted the sky. We gathered together at mom's bedside, Nic seated and I standing, our conversation steeped in fragments of joy and yearning. Within this fragile space, my mother's voice intertwined with the gentle plea directed at our faithful canine companion to go with grandma (me). And then, a question arose from deep within me, trembling on my lips and yearning for an answer beyond reason.

Later that day, I dared to ask her, "Who am I?" my voice tender and uncertain. A moment of silence swelled between us, heavy with infinite possibilities. At last, her response pierced the stillness, unabashedly honest. "You're my mother," she declared, her words both reassuring and heartbreaking. Emboldened, I pressed on, inquiring about the presence beside her. Her answer came without hesitation, a fragile thread connecting us. "Your sister," she whispered. Yet, amidst the haze of fading memories, our loyal pup remains a steadfast guardian, remembering her daily.

On 8/14/2022, mom's perception of reality blurred as she believed she had embarked on a picturesque journey to Yosemite with Nic and her friend's family. In her mind, she painted vivid landscapes of its beauty, unaware of the confines of her room.

A week later, on 8/21/2022, we celebrated mom's birthday with heartfelt gestures. We showered her with chocolates, caramels, vibrant flowers, and a floating balloon. Amidst the intimacy of her bedroom, we witnessed a flicker of joy illuminating her features, a fleeting moment of clarity that warmed our hearts.

On 8/29/22, Gabrielle showered her grandma and surprised our pup with a gorgeous new collar! She even successfully convinced grandma to come to the living room, which was a significant achievement!

Then, the following day, on 8/30/2022, a significant transition unfolded as we entered the realm of home hospice. The first order of business entailed arranging a hospital bed and essential supplies like oxygen tanks and a condenser. Hospice now assumed responsibility for providing necessary items such as pull-ups, wipes, fall pads, nebulizers, medications, cleansers, and antiseptics. Adjusting to the hospital bed proved challenging for mom, as any form of change disrupted her delicate equilibrium. However, we assured her it would offer greater comfort for her and Nicolette, sparing us from straining our backs during lifts. Mom despised the hospital bed, and I questioned myself about introducing it into the home.

Additionally, a nurse now visits us once a week, offering assistance and support. Knowing that we can reach out to hospice at any time, whether through calls or texts, eases our minds, alleviating some of the weight we carry.

On 9/05/2022, Gabrielle dedicated an hour to tending to mom's well-being. She showered her and lovingly washed her hair. In a moment of confusion, mom turned to me, her question lingering,

"So I didn't need a shower today?" With gentle reassurance, I informed her that Gabrielle had provided her with a soothing shower accompanied by a thorough hair wash and that she looked beautiful.

Mom in 1960's

CHAPTER EIGHT

"FADING HEALTH AND FRAGILE STEPS"

On the memorable morning of 10/16/2022, a day that will forever be etched into my heart, my mother awoke from her slumber at the gentle hour of 11:30 am. The sunlight streamed through the curtains, painting the room with a soft glow. As she savored her breakfast, a delicate mix of flavors dancing on her tongue, little did she know that this would be a day filled with ups and downs.

But destiny had other plans, as my mother found herself succumbing to the embrace of sleep once again, the exhaustion taking hold of her fragile body. Lunch was served, a feast for her eyes, yet her appetite remained untouched. With each passing hour, the shadows of slumber grew longer, embracing her like a heavy blanket.

And so, on 10/26/2022, the night whispered loneliness as my dear mother couldn't recall having her evening meal. The day had started with a late breakfast at 11:00 am, each bite offering a brief respite from the clouded haze that enveloped her mind. At 3:00 pm, she indulged in a modest portion of a pastrami sandwich, a mere morsel of satisfaction. The evening unfolded with the symphony of ribs, mashed potatoes, and garlic bread at 6:30 pm, a fleeting moment of gustatory pleasure. To cap off the night, a sweet indulgence of ice cream and cookies at 9:00 pm painted a temporary smile on her weary face.

But time moved on, and so did my mother's lucidity. On the sorrowful date of 10/27/2022, October, I awoke her from her slumber and guided her to the bathroom. A bewildered expression graced her face as she asked, "What am I doing?" The weight of this moment weighed heavily on my heart. Later that afternoon, as I tended to her, replacing the gauze on her delicate hand, she inquired whether I had heard from the doctor about her condition. My heart ached as I whispered, "No, there's nothing more we can do." The decline in her mental faculties became more apparent by the day, a haunting reality that I struggled to comprehend. It is a devastating sight, an experience that scars my soul with profound sadness.

On 11/01/2022, in a moment of fleeting clarity, my mother spoke words of love and admiration, mistaking me for her mother. She praised the dedication and selflessness of her imaginary daughter, a talented ballerina whose dreams were shattered by a cruel twist of knee injuries. Memories of a childhood spent cherishing animals swirled in her fragmented mind. I uttered no words, overwhelmed with emotion, as I sat beside her and let tears silently flow. It was a bittersweet conversation, perhaps the last semblance of coherence I would ever have with her, though she remained unaware of my true identity.

Two days later, the world continued its relentless march. On 11/03/2022, as I roused my mother from her slumber at 11:00 a.m., I discovered a surprising absence—she had removed her pull-up.

Confusion and concern churned within me, but I reassured myself as I felt the secureness of the bed beneath my touch, a temporary respite from the worries that plagued me.

Then, on the somber eve of 11/04/2022, I returned from the park only to be greeted by my mom with a heavy heart. The words tumbled from her lips, carrying news that shattered the fragile shell of our existence. The police had come knocking at our door, bearing the burden of sorrow. Nic, my dear daughter, had been involved in a tragic accident. The weight of those words settled heavily upon my shoulders as if the world itself had shifted beneath my feet. In that moment, time stood still, and the air grew heavy with an unspoken fear.

In her confusion, my mother had reached out to our compassionate neighbor Erin, who hastened to our side without hesitation. And then, in her desperate attempt to seek solace, my mother called my other daughter, Gabrielle, and her boyfriend, whose impeccable legal prowess adorned him with the aura of a true legal luminary. But these were mere fabrications of my mother's tangled mind, a desperate grasp for familiarity in a world that was slipping away.

During this chaos, the truth remained suspended, the reality of the accident looming like a dark cloud. Yet, I couldn't bear to shatter my mother's fragile grasp on reality, to tell her the true extent of the tragedy that had befallen our family. And so, I sat there, absorbing the weight of the false information she spoke, my heart aching with the weight of undisclosed grief.

Our home became a realm of bittersweet moments, caught between fragmented memories and the sad truth. Each day, I found myself slipping further into a tangle of emotions: sadness, resilience, and an unyielding devotion to protect my mother's fragile thread of sanity.

In this sea of confusion and heartache, I learned the true meaning of strength. I embraced the role thrust upon me, the identity converging with my mother's. And in those moments, as I held her frail hand, I realized that love transcends the boundaries of time and comprehension.

Onward, we walked, navigating the labyrinth of my mother's mind, witnessing the fading light of recognition and the beauty of fleeting moments of clarity. And in those darkened corridors, I clung to the stories she wove, the fragments of truth entwined within her tangled memories. Though the truth eluded her, her words held treasures of a life lived fully, of dreams chased and cherished in the depths of her being.

On the impactful date of 11/9/2022, my mother's journey took a new turn as she was prescribed a new medication, Seroquel, with hopes of finding some respite from the tumultuous symptoms she had been experiencing. With a glimmer of hope, she took her first dose and drifted into a night of peaceful slumber. However, the morning was challenging as she struggled to wake from her newfound tranquility. Confusion washed over her as she said, "Why can't I hear?" My heart tightened with fear at her distress, urging her to sit up and speak, hoping the sound of her voice would bring reassurance. The weight of her anxiety and the elusive grip of hallucinations left us both feeling vulnerable. She was ok after the bathroom trip. The medication was so strong for her that she went back to sleep at 12 and remained asleep for the entire night. Days merged into a disorienting loop as if trapped within the confines of an unchanging reality. On 11/12/2022, we faced another day marked by explosive bouts of diarrhea and a dwindling appetite that made it painfully apparent that her stomach problems were escalating. Each passing day presented a new challenge, testing the limits of her endurance and my resilience.

With the regularity of clockwork, on the significant date of 11/20/2022, I embarked on the bimonthly ritual of clipping my mother's nails. As I delicately trimmed her fingernails, anxiety emanated from her, its suffocating grip palpable. This wave of distress enveloped both of us, filling the room with a heavy sadness that weighed upon my heart.

On 11/22/2022, mom was spending more time asleep and eating less. The nurse visited and started administering oxygen. Nic and I monitored mom's blood pressure and pulse ox daily, which remained steady at 92. Mom's declining health filled our hearts with a deep sense of sorrow and helplessness as we watched her condition worsen with each passing day.

On 11/25/2022, I coaxed my mother to venture out of the confines of her room, hoping to offer her a change of scenery in the living room. The silence hung heavy in the air, a stark reminder of the emptiness that engulfed our days. To gauge her thoughts, I asked if she found solace in the quiet. Her reply pierced the stillness, "No if it's quiet, I think I am dead." The weight of those words settled upon us, a testament to the despair that coexisted with every waking moment.

Days blurred together, and on 11/30/2022, our nurse's presence brought a sense of urgency. The task of awakening my mother proved to be prolonged, the depths of her slumber refusing to release its hold. It took 20 minutes to rouse her that day. Concern heightened as the nurse detected rattling sounds clinging to her lungs. Swift action followed, with a nebulizer treatment and the administration of oxygen. The toll of the day left my mother extremely disoriented, her connection to the world slipping further away.

As November's final days unfolded, my mother's overwhelmed nature became unmistakable. On 12/06/2022, she mustered the strength to ask if anyone else would be present that day. The presence of multiple individuals, whether it be the doctor, the caregivers, or the bathers, became an overwhelming prospect for her already burdened mind. The delicate balance of her existence teetered as she navigated the complexities of daily interactions. The weight of multiple presences seemed to multiply her anxieties, leaving her feeling overwhelmed and vulnerable in the face of these seemingly ordinary encounters.

I realized the delicate tightrope we walked, balancing my mother's comfort and well-being with the necessities of her care. Each decision and action was carefully measured to minimize the weight, the burden that pressed upon her frail frame. And so, as the days passed, a mix of emotions swirled within me. The simplicity of routine was tinged with sadness, acknowledging the inevitable decline that encumbered my mother's journey. Yet, during the struggles and challenges, moments of clarity emerged like rays of sunlight through the darkest clouds.

With all its beauty and pain, the circle of life bound us together inextricably, reminding me of the fragility and preciousness of each passing day. As we navigated this journey, hand in hand, the weight of my love and devotion steadied us both, providing a steady anchor amid the storm.

CHAPTER NINE

"CHRISTMAS SHADOWS AND MOMENTS OF LIGHT"

On 12/11/22, Gabrielle's birthday brought a bittersweet moment as she sat with her grandma, who lovingly recounted the story of the day Gabrielle entered the world. As memories flooded back, mom nostalgically recalled how she had prepared a generous spread of fried chicken for the boys when she returned home from the hospital. In that poignant moment, Gabrielle realized the precious connection between her birth and the cherished memories shared between generations. The tender exchange of stories served as a poignant reminder of the enduring love and family ties that bind them together across time and space.

As the two souls shared a tender embrace, my heart swelled with pride and gratitude. During this moment of familial connection, my dear mother felt compelled to share an intimate story that held the key to a cherished memory.

"With the same love that envelops us today, my child," my mother's voice quivered slightly, "I recall the day you graced this world." My mom was telling the story of my birth, not her granddaughter, Gabrielle.

The room felt suspended between the past and the present as my mother recounted the tender moments surrounding my birth. With each carefully chosen word, she kept making memories. I closed my eyes, allowing her voice to transport me back to that momentous day when my journey of motherhood began.

A heartfelt gasp escaped Gabrielle's lips, accompanied by a glimmer of recognition in her eyes. She realized with a whispered realization that it was her own origin story unfolding before her. In that instant, the connection between generations became tangible - a bridge forged through the power of storytelling and the shared bonds of love.

On 12/19/22, mom started experiencing sundowning around 7:30 pm each day, followed by prolonged wakefulness into the late evening hours. Despite the anti-anxiety medications being administered, their effectiveness gradually waned, leaving mom in a state of restlessness and wakefulness during the nighttime hours. Hours would tick by, the hands of the clock spinning in endless circles, while she remained awake within the depths of the night. The once-effective anti-anxiety medications failed to soothe her restless mind, leaving her trapped in a tangled labyrinth of forgotten memories and bewilderment.

The weight of this realization pressed heavily upon my heart, urging me to seek solace in the company of our nurse. She arrived on 12/20/2022, bearing both concern and gentle reassurance. It was then that the cruel reality of my mother's physical decline became unmistakable. She had lost a staggering 4 pounds, her frail frame struggling to retain the vitality slipping through her fingers like sand.

With trembling hands, I was entrusted with administering breathing treatments, a routine demanding diligence and compassion. Each day, without fail, I would confront the fragility of her spirit as her body wheezed and struggled for the precious breath of life. In those tender moments, when the rhythm of her breathing became intertwined with my own, I was caught between a fragile hope and the sad acceptance of reality.

Yet, the passage of time proved to be an unyielding force, unrelenting in its pursuit to unravel the fabric of our lives. On 12/23/2022, the world seemed to hold its breath as another chapter unfolded in our tumultuous journey. In a haunting echo of vulnerability, my mother attempted to navigate her way into the bathroom alone, only to lose her footing and fall. Panic surged through my veins as the sound of her frail body hitting the ground reverberated through the walls.

In that moment of chaos and fear, Nicolette and I rushed to her side, our hearts pounding in unison. Together, we lifted her fragile form from the cold, unforgiving tiles and cradled her in our arms. There were no visible signs of trauma, no glaring indication that her fall had brought forth irrevocable harm. Relief mingled with concern as we awaited the nurse's arrival, due to assess the situation in a mere half hour.

As we waited, the weight of the unknown hung heavy in the air. We knew that even a seemingly trivial incident could carry unforeseen consequences for my mother's already delicate state. It was during this anxious pause that I discovered a deeply primal impulse fueled by love - the fierce desire to protect and care for my mother, to shield her from the cruel blows life had dealt her.

To ease her daily struggles, a bedside commode was ordered - a device meant to bring a modicum of convenience to my mother's diminishing independence. Yet, as I gazed upon this foreign contraption standing at the ready, I couldn't help but question its efficacy. Would my mother be able to comprehend its purpose? Would her deteriorating mind grasp the concept and the mechanics required? It was a conundrum that tugged at my heart, exposing the cracks in our once unbreakable bond.

Amidst the depths of our despair, a glimmer of light managed to pierce through the looming darkness. 12/25/2022, Christmas day, arrived with a promise of respite and warmth. Nicolette gently guided our frail mother to the living room chair with her unwavering patience and tender touch. The love that emanated from her was a beacon of hope, a reminder that even amidst the storms of life, moments of pure connection and joy still awaited us.

As the presents sat in a colorful array, anticipation coursed through our veins. With each carefully unwrapped gift, laughter and tears intertwined, mingling in a symphony of emotions. The moment's beauty lay not in the material possessions but in the shared love and the fleeting respite from the burdens we carried. It was a reminder that, no matter how unyielding the challenges, the bonds of family had the power to heal and provide solace in times of darkness.

The echoes of my mother's words resounded in the room like a gentle melody carrying the weight of love. "Nicolette is the best at taking care of me," she often said, her voice filled with admiration and gratitude. Their bond was unbreakable, a testament to Nicolette's unwavering love and devotion. It was a sentiment that touched our hearts, reminding us of the power of familial connection.

As the day wore on, the atmosphere shifted, casting a melancholic shadow over our hearts. Gabrielle and her boyfriend joined us for dinner, hoping to bring a glimmer of joy to my mother's eyes. We tried everything - telling jokes and recounting happy memories, but her spirit remained low, almost empty. Her mental faculties were slipping away with each passing day, her once vibrant mind now a mere flicker of its former glory. The weight of witnessing her decline on this Christmas day weighed heavily upon us, casting a veil of sadness upon the festivities.

12/27/2022 dawned with a heaviness that seemed to permeate the air. My mother's weakened state became ever more pronounced, her tiredness consuming her fragile frame. The persistent wheezing was a haunting reminder of the battles she fought within herself. During a conversation with our hospice nurse, the harsh reality of the situation was laid bare. She gently explained that my mother's condition would only worsen from this point on, a prognosis that filled us with a profound sense of helplessness.

That day became an inflection point when fatigue threatened to overtake our weary souls. Exhausted from the ceaseless care we provided, Nicolette and I were teetering on the edge. Each task, no matter how seemingly small, demanded an immense amount of strength. Changing my mother's pull-up required delicate maneuvering, as her once-cooperative limbs now required manual guidance. It was a heartrending sight, watching her struggle to comprehend the simplest of instructions, a testament to the unforgiving march of time.

1/1/2023 heralded a new year, yet our hearts remained heavy with the burden of our reality.

On 1/7/2023, stepping into my mother's room, I found her sitting on the toilet, her frail form a testament to her diminishing strength. Concern filled my voice as I asked if she needed help. In her clouded mind, she whispered words that reflected the distress she bore within. "Lock the doors; there's rioting going on outside. Don't you hear the gunfire?"

With gentle reassurance, I tried to alleviate her fears, reminding her that we were safe and surrounded by a community that cared for one another. A soothing melody of classical music played in the background, an attempt to replace the news cycle that often inundated her thoughts. Tonight, Nancy Pelosi appeared on a program discussing the insurrection, and in her confusion, my mother believed it was unfolding before her very eyes.

In this journey of love and caregiving, emotions ran deep. The drama unfolded with each passing day as we witnessed the gradual fading of a once vibrant soul. Yet, during the hardship, glimmers of resilience and love persisted, reminding us to cherish the moments, no matter how fleeting. We were determined to face the challenges with a blend of sorrow and strength, grasping hope like a lifeline in the face of the unknown.

CHAPTER TEN

"THE FALL"

On the fateful day of 1/08/2022, the weight of the situation hung heavily in the air as our dear hospice nurse made her visit. The stark reality of my mother's deteriorating health revealed itself through her distressingly low blood pressure reading of 96/53. A heart-wrenching moment forced us to confront the painful truth: nothing more could be done. As we mustered our strength, we coaxed my mom into standing up, a simple act imbued with the gravity of the situation. It was a poignant and tearful scene that etched into our collective memory.

On 1/10/2023, I took a short respite break, leaving Nicolette with detailed instructions for our dedicated caregiver. As mom's care needs evolved, it became a collaborative effort, requiring the presence of both the caregiver and Nicolette or myself to ensure mom's well-being. The daily routine included providing her with fresh clothes after using the bathroom, administering medication, preparing her breakfast, which consisted of an egg cheese bacon bowl and toast, and ensuring she had her preferred hot chocolate. Mom's changing taste preferences and need for engagement were noted, along with responsibilities such as laundry, changing bedding, dishwasher duties, and caring for the family dog. The intricate balance of care highlighted the importance of attentive support and understanding as we navigated each day's challenges together.

As days slipped by, the gravity of the situation deepened.

1/11/2023 brought with it the painful realization of my mother's diminishing ability to swallow. This mundane act of sustenance now required painstaking precautions. We sliced everything into quarter pieces, fearing any potential choking hazards. The nature of her condition added an emotional layer to our caregiving routine, a constant reminder of her vulnerability and fragility.

On 1/16/2023, my daughter, Gabrielle, went on a work trip in San Francisco and brought her dog and a newly adopted kitten for a weekend stay. The unexpected presence of the lively kitten proved to be a blessing in disguise. It brought joy and solace to my mother's weary eyes. The furry companion curled up on her lap, offering fleeting moments of comfort and connection that briefly lifted the heavy emotional burden we were all carrying. The kitten comfortably slept on my mom each night, bringing mom such pure joy. I am forever grateful for that kitten whom mom had renamed.

We couldn't deny that new challenges unfolded before our eyes. The emotional rollercoaster we rode on seemed never-ending, with moments of profound tenderness intertwined with heartbreaking difficulties. Yet, amidst the profound sadness, there was a subtle awareness of the preciousness of time spent with my ailing mother. Each passing moment became an invaluable gift, treasured and held onto tightly.

The following day, 1/17/2023, was incredibly odd and unsettling, filled with a whirlwind of emotions and unexpected events. The atmosphere in our home was heavy with worry as my mother's behavior deviated from her usual routine. She barely touched her meals and refused to take her usual afternoon nap. Something wasn't right, and I couldn't shake off the unease in the air.

Oh, how I wished for a reprieve from the anxiety of administering my mother's nighttime medication. I silently hoped that tonight would be different, that I wouldn't have to grapple with my nerves and fear of making a mistake. With her exhaustion, I had hoped she would find solace in a deep sleep, allowing her body to heal.

However, fate had other plans in store for us. It was a Tuesday, a brand new day that would soon become etched in our memories for all the wrong reasons. In the early morning, my daughter Nicolette abruptly woke up at 4:11 am, jolted by the piercing sound of our mother's life-alert charm necklace. Panic raced through her veins as she hurried downstairs, only to find my mother sprawled on the floor, her frailty and vulnerability exposed.

Nicolette's frantic shouts reached my ears, and like a bolt of lightning, they jolted me awake from my fitful sleep. Fear gripped my heart as I processed the urgency in her voice. Without a moment's hesitation, I grabbed my phone and hastily dialed 911, requesting immediate medical help. The operator's calm yet urgent voice provided a temporary lifeline amidst the chaos that had suddenly engulfed our lives. Mom had fallen, and she sustained significant injuries: a fractured hip and shoulder. In the ambulance, she was administered morphine, a bittersweet relief that dulled her senses, granted her a temporary respite, and eased her pain. Once in the Emergency Department, as her body adjusted to its effects, her blood pressure abruptly dropped, setting off alarm bells within the medical staff. In a desperate attempt to stabilize her, they decided to administer ketamine, a potent anesthetic that would allow her to endure the necessary treatments, procedures, and pain management.

The combination of drugs left my mother in an altered state, caught in an alternate reality where the boundaries between dreams and consciousness blurred. As I lay beside her, the hospital bed sagging slightly under our weight, I couldn't help but feel her anguish and confusion. Her words pierced through the fog of medication, her voice laced with vulnerability as she asked if she should move over to make room for me. With a gentle touch, I reassured her I was fine, balled up next to her, reminding her gently of her condition. I reminded her about her broken hip and emphasized that I was perfectly content being right by her side. Her face wrinkled with concern and relief, and in that tender moment, I realized the depth of her trust in me. I couldn't help but feel a surge of love and gratitude for the opportunity to be there for her in a time of such vulnerability. Mom kept asking me when we could go home. My heart shattered.

Amid the layers of worry and confusion, a flicker of unexpected humor momentarily broke through the tension. I asked my mother to describe her pain on a scale of one to ten, a common medical assessment. However, instead of offering a number, she simply replied, "Pink." It was a peculiar response that brought a smile to my face amidst the otherwise somber atmosphere. At that moment, I realized the power of laughter was a balm for the wounded soul, even during turmoil.

When the orthopedic doctors informed me that surgery was not viable due to my mother's advanced dementia, without surgery, she would be unable to walk again. Subsequently, another physician and a social worker arrived in the emergency room and recommended placing mom on hospice care, given her Do Not Resuscitate (DNR) status. I consented to this decision and remained by my mother's side until a hospice room became available, a process that took approximately 16 hours. This date marked the final occasion I heard my mother's voice.

I contacted my brothers to share the news and encouraged them to speak with mom and express anything they wished her to know. Although the realization that she might not return home with us had not crossed my mind, it incited a chapter of uncertainty.

The line crackled with anticipation as I listened to the silence on the other end of the call. Time seemed to stretch infinitely as I awaited their response, yearning for their empathetic voices, craving the shared burden of this heavy reality. Finally, their words poured forth, a mix of shock, concern, and a shared determination to be there for our mother. I found a glimmer of hope in their voices, a reminder that we were not alone in this tumultuous journey.

Subconsciously, as I reached out to my brothers, I secretly held onto a sliver of hope, a thread of belief that our mother would soon return home with us, her familiar presence gracing our lives once more. It never occurred to me that this plea for communication was also a plea for closure, a desperate attempt to impart any unspoken messages or hidden truths to our mother's fragile spirit.

Little did I know then that fate had other plans for us. This day, this unexpected and catastrophic event would mark the beginning of a path we were unprepared to tread. In the days ahead, we would face the challenges of rehabilitation, the intricacies of medical decisions, and the harsh reality of our limitations. But for now, all I could do was hold on to the treasured memories, the love, and the unyielding hope that carried us through each passing day.

The reality of the situation hit us with an almost tangible force. A cadre of medical professionals, their serious expressions and efficient movements underscoring the severity of the situation greeted us. It was then that we learned the true extent of my mother's injuries—a fractured shoulder and hip, two injuries that would test her resilience and our collective strength in the days to come.

Following a prolonged and emotionally taxing day, I arrived home at 7:00 pm. Seeking solace and closeness to mom, I went to her room and chose to sleep in her hospital bed, cherishing the familiarity and comfort it provided during this challenging time.

Yet, even with these fleeting moments of respite, a wave of guilt crashed over me, threatening to consume my every thought. It was a guilt born out of a simple and human wish – the desire for my mother to regain her health and return to a semblance of normalcy. In the depths of my heart, I yearned for her to be whole again, to reclaim the familiarity and comfort of the home we had so cherished. But now, this wish haunted me, for I feared it had unwittingly cast a shadow over our lives, leading us down an unforeseen path.

CHAPTER ELEVEN

"MY HERO IS GONE"

The following day, 1/18/2023, I found myself back at the hospital. My mom lay heavily sedated, her frail body mouthing the word "pain." The medical team decided to administer a booster of morphine to alleviate her suffering. It was a heartbreaking sight.

Later that day, my older daughter, Gabrielle, arrived to lend her support. As she witnessed the gravity of the situation, her eyes filled with tears. Nicolette, the steadfast caregiver of my mother and my beloved daughter, who had been by my mom's side for the past four years, also joined us. Her unwavering devotion was evident as she brought mom's favorite blankets and a Vermont teddy bear adorned with butterfly wings. It was a small gesture, but it held so much meaning.

As the hours passed, the realization sank in that my mom's kidneys were starting to shut down. A wave of helplessness washed over me, and an illogical need to stay overnight in her room overwhelmed my senses. It was as if staying close to her would shield her from the unfolding tragedy.

Attempting to take a brief respite from the hospital, I went home for a much-needed shower on 1/19/2023. The minutes felt like hours as I anxiously awaited updates from my mom's nurse. When I returned, I saw that her eyes had fluttered open. Still, her unwillingness to eat persisted. Nicolette, unyielding in her support, returned to provide a comforting presence for the remainder of the day. She witnessed firsthand my mom's frailty and the toll it was taking on me.

Later in the day, I relieved Nicolette for several hours. It was during this time that I experienced a bittersweet moment. My mom, defying her weakened state, accepted two bites of applesauce. It was a fleeting victory, a tiny glimmer of hope amidst the dark clouds. But just as quickly as the triumph appeared, it faded away. My mom began to spike high fevers, her body succumbing to the battle within. Instinctively, I chose non-invasive measures to soothe her, gently applying cold compresses to her forehead. It was a small act of protection against the encroaching turmoil.

On 1/20/2023, I stayed overnight in her room, assuming the role of a silent guardian. Every passing hour was a reminder of the impending loss, but I refused to let go. I found myself back in Room 8.21 at the hospital, which shared the same number as my mom's birthday. It was an oddly coincidental detail that added to the moment's weight. As the hospice physicians entered, their words echoed through the room, resonating with a chilling finality. "She will pass away here," they said. It was at that moment that the harsh reality hit me like a ton of bricks—my mom was not going to come home with us. The news left me overwhelmed and seeking solace in the familiarity of home.

Leaving Nicolette, a constant source of support for my mom, to be with her grandmother, I retreated to the comforts of our house. I couldn't stay away for long, as I longed to be near my mom in her final moments. Nicolette stayed with her, reading to her for hours and playing her favorite music, creating a soothing environment filled with love and familiarity. Each update I received brought mixed emotions as I learned that my mom was now catheterized—a symbolic tether to a reality slipping away.

Returning to the hospital, I joined Nicolette and my mom. In a deeply touching moment, amidst my declarations of love, my mom mouthed, "I love you too." Mom knew who I was and responded to my voice. It was a bittersweet reminder of the strength of our bond as she recognized me despite the hardships she faced. She was never alone with the support of Nicolette, Gabrielle, and myself. We filled the room with poetry, celebrating her life on the edge of death. Her favorite music played softly in the background, creating a farewell symphony.

As if the moment's weight weren't heavy enough, my eldest brother braved treacherous snowstorms to be with us, bringing relief and anxiety. His arrival at 10:00 pm marked a bittersweet reunion, a family united in the face of impending loss. I am forever grateful that my brother arrived safely.

1/21/2023 marked a day of gathering and somber anticipation. My brother, Nicolette, my older daughter, Gabrielle, and I assembled at the hospital, knowing that my mom was now nonresponsive and on the edge of her last moments. Our sincere hope was for her to find peace and not be afraid as she transitioned. Gabrielle, after expressing her love and bidding her goodbyes, left the hospital, leaving us in hushed anticipation of an imminent farewell.

Examining my mom's feet beneath the layers of blankets revealed the telltale signs of mottling—a poignant testament to her body's gradual surrender. It was a sobering realization that her time with us was rapidly ending. At 2:00 pm, I asked Nicolette to leave, sparing her the anguish of witnessing the final breaths. Her parting tear marked the beginning of my mom's transition. This phenomenon of shedding a single tear is known as lacrima mortis. The tears are not of emotional crying but of saying goodbye.

Amid the agonal breathing that filled the room, my brother and I sat vigil by my mom's side. His gentle hand caressed her forehead while mine clenched hers, trying to anchor her against the forces eagerly awaiting her departure. On that dark day of my life, on 1/21/2023, at 4:50 pm, my mom took her last breath, signaling the painful reality of our irrevocable loss. A cry escaped my brother, confirming the depth of our sorrow. I asked my brother, "Is that it?" Mom is just gone now?

Reluctant to let go, we lingered in the room for an hour, gathering mementos that held memories and the essence of my mom. The blankets that provided warmth, the Vermont teddy bear she cherished, and even the nightgown that had been ceremoniously cut away upon our arrival now carried a weight of significance.

At that moment, the room felt heavy with the weight of grief and the lingering presence of my mom. We packed our belongings, heartache mirroring every item we carefully placed into bags.

As we walked out of Room 8.21 for the last time, a sense of emptiness settled in, replacing the bustling energy that had once filled those walls. Outside, the world continued to spin, oblivious to the profound loss we had just experienced. It was a stark reminder that life moves forward, even when our hearts ache to hold on to the past. We were left to grapple with the void left by my mom's absence, trying to find our footing in this altered reality.

In the days and weeks that followed, we navigated the complicated process of grieving, each of us finding solace in our way. Memories of my mom punctuated our thoughts, bringing comfort and pain to equal measure. We reminisced about her infectious laughter, her unwavering love, and the imprint she had left on our lives.

The healing journey is slow and unpredictable, with ups and downs that mirror the unpredictable nature of grief. But amidst the sorrow, we found strength in one another and in the legacy my mom had left behind. She had taught us the value of resilience, compassion, and the power of a life lived fully.

We carry her spirit in her absence, cherishing the memories and lessons she bestowed upon us. We face the future without her but are determined to honor her memory and continue the legacy she has created.

In Room 8.21, we said our final farewells to my mom, witnessing the fragility of life and the resilience of love. We will forever carry the pain of that day in our hearts as a testament to the profound impact she had on our lives. As we stumbled into the unknown, we held onto the lessons learned during her final days. We cherished the moments of love and connection, recognizing the fragility of life and the importance of treasuring those we hold dear. And, though the ache of loss would always remain, we found solace in the bond that tied us together—a bond strengthened by the indelible mark my mom had left on our souls.

Nicolette, my beloved daughter, dedicated four years to caring for my mother. She became a steadfast pillar of support for me, especially when I questioned my resilience. She never left my side, guiding and encouraging me when I felt too weak to move forward. She brought a glimmer of hope into my life during the darkest times. Today, I am sharing her journey through Nicolette's words.

NICOLETTE'S WORDS

Nicolette's Diary

February 11th, 2020:

Having my grandma live with us these past months has already been such an enlightening experience. It's all new to me, this caregiving thing. But I do feel a renewed sense of purpose with this responsibility. This unique task of tending to my grandma is greater than me. It feels comforting to have another maternal figure in my life, especially one I've always admired, only now the tables have turned. Spending quality time with her is imperative as much as it is amusing. Whenever she starts her familiar tales, I sit attentively, pretending I've never heard them. She finds joy in sharing her stories, particularly about her adventures abroad. She delivers each one like a well-practiced monologue, which never impresses me. You can see the excitement in her foggy eyes while reliving these moments, which brings me more joy than she could ever know. Listening to her various journeys has become one of my favorite pastimes, and I hope to one day recreate these momentous excursions. Her curious sense of wonder is surely rooted in me, and I look forward to diving into that part of myself even more.

May 11th, 2020:

No one said this would be easy. A few nights ago, we rushed our dog to the emergency room. We got her the proper medication, and she is on her way to recovery. Then, last night, grandma took a fall. Thankfully, she was unharmed, but it terrified me. On top of all that, just before Mother's Day, mom ended up in the ER. It feels like a relentless cycle of hardships and worries. When will it ever end? I'm thankful everyone has made it out unscathed throughout these chaotic times. Adapting during these new pandemic times has been more than a challenge. We're all just getting the hang of things. I feel completely isolated, as I'm sure everyone else does. I'm trying to make the best of a horrible situation and, more than anything— keep my grandma safe. Focusing on my family is my diversion tactic. Although being the "strong" one for them— especially for my mom, is exhausting, it distracts me from my debilitating anxiety, as well as my disappointment. Friendships have changed, and I feel deserted, left to continue my caregiving role with no outside support. I am longing for any positivity to come from this. Karma's real, right?

August 21st, 2020:

It's grandma's birthday today. This year, we're celebrating at home to keep her safe. I made up a goodie bag of all her favorite candies, which the dog hand-delivered for her when she woke up. Made it the best we possibly could for her. We spent the day relaxing and having lots of laughs, having her favorite meal from the finest cuisines, AKA Outback. Her cheerfulness and joy throughout her face ensured me that she was having an enjoyable birthday. We topped the day off with a delicious cake that she devoured. She deserves any moment in which she can feel special and appreciated. After all, 85 is no easy feat.

August 31st, 2020:

When grandma asked for lunch today, I quickly made a plate for her, as she hates to wait. However, when I went to her room, she had gone to the bathroom and had no pants. Concerned, I offered my help, but she resisted, asking for a few minutes alone. When I returned, she had undressed entirely, leaving me bewildered. Nothing seems to make sense anymore. I continue to fight with myself to understand. I could tell she was puzzled about why she'd done that, and that makes me sadder than anything. Seeing the confusion in her eyes made me pause and re-conceptualize this situation through a different lens. She has no idea what's going on, and my heart aches. At times like these, I just wish I knew how I could help her better. I simply informed her that lunch was ready and guided her in getting dressed. I continued as best I could without breaking the strong and resilient character I often play.

October 12th, 2020:

You know when people say some days are harder than others? This is one of those days. I know it sounds dramatic, but I feel like a prisoner. This ever-looming "stuck" feeling is beginning to decay my once ambitious and charismatic self. My mother and I are battling to find a balance. I'm on a strict time clock to get home and tend to my duties when I leave the house. Then, when I'm home, I'm still on a strict time clock and tend to my duties. The heavy weight of my mom's pain deflecting onto me doesn't make my responsibility for my grandma any lighter. I try as much as humanly possible to be compassionate, but sometimes, you just gotta scream into your pillow or go on a run until you can't feel your legs.

March 6th, 2021:

I often attributed my loneliness to the necessary precautions and isolation during this pandemic. But it extended far beyond that. As a caregiver for my 85-year-old grandma, along with managing my autoimmune disease, I've had to be extra cautious and vigilant this past year. Unexpectedly, I've undergone a significant physical transformation amidst the challenges, losing 55 pounds. If there was one thing I could control, it would be becoming a healthier human. I not only feel like my previous self but, in many ways, a renewed and improved version. Keeping up with my new physical habits and form has helped me maintain a positive outlet. I just wish that these effects also took place in my brain. No matter how fit I become, the mental anguish is still there.

March 7th, 2021:

Dealing with a flooded toilet has become a new annoyance in our daily routine. Water splattered everywhere, and grandma seemed to forget to flush. To make matters worse, she struggles to move her middle finger, and basic tasks like locating the trash can elude her memory. These various declinations feel like moments of defeat, shattering my hope of her improving in any way. She carries a tremendous sense of guilt about everything, reinforcing my feelings of guilt. I feel powerless, desperately wanting to help her through this chaotic time. Everything seems to be moving at an alarming pace. For the first time, my mind could comprehend where this was heading, making everything much more dreadful.

June 22nd, 2021:

Mom left for the week, where Morongo awaited her favorite place to get away. We've started taking solo mini-vacations to clear our minds and be free of obligations for a short time. In a silly way, it's also a vacation for my grandma. I think she feels a sense of freedom when there aren't two people micromanaging her all day. Although these periods of solitude are appreciated, they ultimately proved to be fleeting. A few days ago, grandma had a serious accident on the way to her bathroom from the living room. Every time I hear my mom shout, "NIC!" I know something grave has happened. Upon hearing my name in that familiar shriek, I ran downstairs to assist in the aftermath. Depends have now been ordered. Another bathroom accident, which I happily cleaned. These are the types of thoughts that consume me every waking moment. I'm forever yearning to better understand how to prevent and be better prepared for these accidents. When mom departed earlier, it triggered an unexpected surge of emotions within me. I ache for a more positive relationship between us, especially during these arduous times. Though I crave some solitude, I'm also aware that I am now responsible for managing our household. Here's hoping the next three days pass without any major issues. I become less anxious as each day passes during her absence, taking solace in knowing we've made it safely through another day.

One night, grandma shared with me the burdensome memories of her childhood. I was happy that she felt she could confide in me; she needed to get things off her chest. She recounted stories of her mother sending her outside regardless of the weather when she was eight. Meanwhile, her mother would entertain men inside. Despite the circumstances, grandma took on the responsibility of caring for her younger siblings, ensuring they were rested and fed. I can hardly fathom the hardships she endured during her formative years, and that's just one small part of her less-than-pleasant adolescence. It's interesting to me how trauma never leaves you, no matter how old you are. Even at her age and in her declining mental state, the need to get rid of these emotional scars never ceased. She's held on to so much. Her enormous strength continues to inspire me.

June 25th, 2021:

Today was another challenging day with grandma. You can usually gauge how it will go upon her waking up. We made it through the day, but she became restless at bedtime. I put on CNN for her, the only channel she likes to watch, but moments later, she began changing the TV channel. As she is already legally blind, we try to make her routines seamless to ensure her comfort. I said goodnight to her, like I always do, regardless of who puts her to bed. That's something I've always been taught. Always say goodnight and goodbye, then finish strong with an "I love you." You never know if those words might be your last. I put her TV on a timer to ease her worries so she wouldn't have to worry about turning it off or finding the right channel. Her finger issue is getting worse. However, she refuses to wear her brace until she sees the doctor. She claims I can't tell her what to do. I get it, and I do; her shrinking autonomy feels degrading. Unfortunately, this led to a painful night for her as she didn't want to wear the brace, insisting she couldn't bear the pain. It's frustrating because I just want her to be okay and sometimes feel helpless. It can feel lonely going through all of this, and I wish I had more support from friends who would ask how things were going or how she was doing. Most of the time, when I vent, I get little to no feedback. I get it; what do you say to someone when you truly can't comprehend what they're going through? It's almost impossible to be empathetic.

June 30th, 2021:

I find myself in Carlsbad now, a place filled with incredible memories of my grandma. She lived here for 12 years, and I'll always treasure the moments when I visited her by train, especially as a teenager. Every time I traveled South to her, I felt more and more independent. It feels bittersweet to be here without her. I could have chosen any vacation spot, but I deliberately came here. My time for a getaway, and I chose to return to grandma's roots. In my way, I wanted to have one last memory of the person she once was. As I strolled the familiar beach town, I stopped to sit at her favorite bench that overlooks Carlsbad State Beach, reminiscing the times of a once-able grandma basking in the sun. Last night, while sitting on a rooftop deck, I had a chance encounter with two amazing people. The husband happened to be an elder care attorney who praised the care I was giving my grandma. His words, telling me that my angel wings were showing and that I was doing a great thing, touched me deeply. We shared wine and had a pleasant hour-long conversation. It was a brief respite before I returned to reality. I packed up some fish and chips from our favorite place we all used to go to as a family and returned home to a delighted grandma.

July 11th, 2021:

Lately, telling the dog and cat apart has become much more difficult. My grandma is declining both her eyesight and mental state. She's resistant to getting out of bed, has no appetite, and seems disconnected from time. Today, I became frantic when my mom had to shake her several times to wake her up. That has to be my worst nightmare. Thankfully, she was just sleeping deeply, but still. She blinks a lot, seemingly trying to find her focus, and appears very disoriented. She expresses a desire to remain immobile and be a "lump." I reminded her she still had a fight left in her, and she laughed and acknowledged that she knew.

July 12th, 2021:

Today, on the way to physical therapy for her hand, she had an accident. She was in a bad mood throughout the session, and I don't blame her. I would be, too. To make matters worse, someone hit my mom's car on the way there. As for the potty accident, grandma joked that it was practice for me when I would have a baby. That's something she's always wanted, and she frequently asks when I will find myself a husband. I know one of her strongest wishes is to see me get married and have children; I would love more than anything for her to witness that. Despite the day's challenges, we try to find moments of humor to lighten the mood. That's all we can do.

July 13th, 2021:

Grandma had a doctor's appointment today and seemed confused about who had taken her. She believed it was my uncle, who lives in Vermont when it was indeed my mother who had taken her. She continues to have a poor appetite and barely eats. If she doesn't want any food I'm offering, I get her whatever she wants, ensuring she's eaten. However, she did have chicken noodle soup for dinner, which is her favorite. Grandma says cooking is not a big deal; no recipe is too complicated for her. She believes she is the one who makes the soup that I serve her, and each time she has it, she carefully explains the details of her recipe. It's an interesting perspective for her to hold onto. It's heartbreaking to witness someone alive but no longer their true self. It feels like I'm grieving her loss while she's still here. In turn, that makes me more depressed, and then guilt follows. I so badly wish I could detach and constantly be lively for her. It's an endless battle.

July 14th, 2021:

Fortunately, today is one of the better days. She even got up to choose an outfit and showed excitement about breakfast! She started spewing different recipe ideas, and I could again detect that shimmer of light in her cloudy eyes. Seeing her enthusiasm and cooking for her brings joy to my heart, as she so often used to do for us. Every time she visited, she'd make enough chicken parmesan to feed us for months. She'd methodically stick most of it in the freezer and explain how easy a meal can be when it's already prepared. You just have to stick it in the "micro." She expressed gratitude for our presence and support, as she often did, and in turn, I always tell her, "That's what I'm here for."

July 28th, 2021:

My focus and daily routine revolve around grandma. To say she is my main focus is an understatement. Lately, she has been refusing to eat dinner at the designated time, making it hard since she no longer can gauge her hunger. It reminds me of a baby being upset and not knowing whether they are hungry or need a diaper change. When it comes to dementia patients, I've learned having a set schedule helps maintain normality, but when she refuses to eat, I feel overcome with despair. I've organized my entire schedule around her, even running downstairs during my Zoom classes to check in, ensuring she doesn't risk falling again by leaving her room unattended. Whenever I hear a noise from downstairs, I fear she's attempting to complete tasks alone, leaving my mind constantly concerned.

August 12th, 2021:

My birthday was just two days ago. My favorite part about August is that my grandma and I are both Leos. I'm not a massive astrology believer, but I notice our personalities' stark similarities. I look forward to celebrating hers in a little over a week. Later in the day, I went on my usual run to clear my head, and upon getting home, I went to check in on her. Her room is next to the front door, so anytime someone comes in, she swings her door open to see who it is. I think it gives her a sense of power; she is the keeper of this house, and she truly is. I entered her room, and grandma conversed with her brother. He's funny and charming, so I am delighted when I hear them talking. I know he puts her in a cheerful mood. However, as she talked to him, she momentarily forgot who my mother was and what relation that makes me to her. I reminded her that my mother is her daughter, and I am her granddaughter. Most of the time, I don't even correct her anymore; doing so often seems to further her confusion. She continued speaking to her brother, concluding that I must always be right. As long as she knows she's safe, I don't care who she thinks I am.

August 18th, 2021:

She seems to have lost the energy to go to the kitchen. She used to enjoy sneaking snacks, and I would catch her in the act, and then we would both have a good laugh. Sometimes, she would do the same to me, creeping up and attempting to scare me. Now, she remains in bed, lacking the strength to get up. It's a double-edged sword. I don't have to worry about a possible fall or injury from a kitchen utensil, which calms me. It also means I won't see her roaming around the house, displaying her still-able state. I miss these encounters. They brightened my day.

August 21st, 2021:

It's grandma's birthday today! I can't believe she's 86 years old. She's a strong force and has accomplished much in her long life. My aunt sent her a beautiful floral arrangement designed to resemble a cake. Despite her diminished cognitive abilities, she could still appreciate the rich colors and fragrances of the flowers. She shared a detailed story about the delivery man walking past each neighbor's door as they walked outside one after another to feast their eyes on this gorgeous "cake." I found it fascinating that she remembered exactly how the walkway was laid out. These details made the story sound much more believable. I chose one of her favorite dresses to match her exquisite flower cake. The colors aligned perfectly, with lush shades of red and orange. She looked stunning, even if she couldn't see it herself.

October 3rd, 2021:

During dinner, grandma claimed not to remember eating just 20 minutes after finishing her meal, suggesting she hadn't had any supper. It's possible she was joking or trying to coax more food out of me. I can never really tell. I can tell, though, that she's still in there somewhere. Her wit never fails to leave her, and her sharpness prevails through her blurred cognition.

October 6th, 2021:

Today, we got grandma to sit in her favorite chair in the living room while we all gathered around, laughing and joking. These are the small victories I must treasure. Curiosity got the better of me, so I asked her about her vision, wondering if it had improved or worsened. Although it seemed like she was having a solid day, I still take these answers with a grain of salt. Being careful not to upset or confuse her, I sought to know if she could still recognize me or my mom. And then, with a mischievous twinkle in her eye, she dropped this gem: "If there are three people, I can tell them apart. So, if there's someone tall and thin, I know it's not Nic". We all burst into laughter. Grandma is truly a savage, and you can't help but love her for it.

November 10th, 2021:

My morning routine with grandma started with a rather traumatizing incident. I went to wake her up for the day when I found her on the bathroom floor. She said she had been there all night, unable to sleep, and with no recollection of how it happened. It was a stark reminder of why we always encourage her to use the bathroom before bed. We don't want her risking a fall by trying to navigate things on her own. I was frightened that she might be hurt, and the guilt weighed heavily on me. Fortunately, she was fine, just tired and sore. I tucked her back into bed, and she took it easy for the rest of the day. Today was the day I truly grasped that, in these moments, we were powerless. I couldn't watch her all night as she slept, so there was no way of ensuring she wouldn't get up and have another fall. There has to be a solution to keep her in bed throughout the night. We will get her life alert necklace so she can ring us when needed. But she's reluctant to use it, fearing she'll be a bother and lose her independence. I express that nothing she does is of any bother, and I will gladly help her anytime she needs it. We're willing to try anything to maintain peace of mind.

December 29th, 2021:

She's a storyteller, all right. Today, grandma insisted that she saw a mountain lion outside her door late at night. She insisted on warning me about safety, especially for our beloved animals. I knew she couldn't have opened the door because we would have received a notification from our Blink camera, but I question my sanity; she is ever so convincing. The camera notifies us of her movements, which has been essential, as she frequently protests to ask for assistance. It's heartbreaking to witness her mind playing tricks on her, but I try my best to reassure her and keep her feeling safe.

January 1st, 2022:

Caretaking can be exceedingly draining and disheartening. Caring for grandma over the past couple of years has taken its toll. Each year, her dementia worsens. Each month and day, it becomes increasingly taxing for all of us. It's hard to stay hopeful for my future when I know that her future doesn't exist. She often expresses a desire for it to all be over in a somber tone, believing that we would be better off without her. I've noticed these dark thoughts often come at moments when she feels extremely vulnerable. I would most likely feel that way as well. I try to relieve her sadness and joke that I would be eternally bored without her. Thankfully, the holidays are behind us now. She's worse each year, and we strive to make them memorable because we never know if they could be her last. Her imminent end is what shakes me to my core.

March 13th, 2022:

I don't have much to write today because my sadness keeps growing. The noticeable deterioration in less than a year terrifies me. I try to focus on living in the present with her, cherishing the good moments rather than dwelling on the bad. Each morning, as I guide her to the bathroom, the shuffling of her feet slows, revealing her mobility is rapidly worsening. Her apprehension to shower is constant. It takes us longer to complete her routine, which includes going to the bathroom, taking her medicine, changing into fresh clothes, followed by breakfast—yet I remain patient and encouraging. She thanks me for my care, often pondering what I will do once she's no longer here. I have no answer as I can't think of a life without her, but I know that whatever I do, it won't feel as fulfilling without being able to share it all with her.

June 12th, 2022:

My grandma shared with me one of her cherished quotes that she lives by, passed down by a dear family member. It goes, "Don't do anything I wouldn't do, but if you do, name it after me." It's a lighthearted motto that brings a smile to her face and reflects her playful spirit.

October 6th, 2022:

Lately, my grandma often mistakes me for my mom, and I've realized there's no point in correcting her anymore. This has been a routine occurrence for over a year now. Despite everything, she is still my best friend. I am grateful to have someone I can talk to whenever I need them. Even with her dementia, she continues to offer invaluable advice with a no-nonsense, brutally honest approach. The wisest words of wisdom come from a true icon. She is my rock, and although she may not fully comprehend it, I regularly express my gratitude. Anything I can do to remind her that she is just as treasured as she once was before her brain became dominated by this disease.

November 28th, 2022:

Grandma got her vaccine, and she's been fairly sick. I haven't been able to spend much time with her since she's been bedridden and unwell, and I miss her. Thankfully, later in the day, she started to feel better after a high fever and soreness, which was a relief. When I came home to make her dinner, she was inspecting the chicken enchiladas out of curiosity, even though she said she could wait for dinner. We were only gone for 15 minutes, and while I understand her need for control, it's frustrating when she somehow manages to sneak out when we're not around. I'd do anything to evade another accident or fall. I tried offering various options, but she declined them all and expressed disappointment with the limited options. Sometimes, it feels like nothing I do is "good enough." I know not to take anything personally anymore, but I'm human. I wish I could step inside her aching mind to figure out how to help her better. Despite these little frustrations, I'm grateful she can still walk to the kitchen on a good day. That is worth celebrating today.

December 13th, 2022:

This holiday season feels overwhelmingly somber. The shadowy cloud that's been looming over us is growing vastly darker. Grandma's sense of recognition is completely decayed, as is her eyesight. Both of us struggle to find the motivation to get out of bed in the morning, but I have to push myself to do it because she relies on me for care. Being deeply depressed myself and seeing how much she is also suffering makes it even harder to pretend to be cheerful for everyone else. I've been drowning in this grief and anguish for a while now, but it's becoming unmanageable. My mom notices something is wrong and urges me to seek help, whether going to the emergency room or talking to someone. I long for a sense of warmth and comfort, a simple hug when I express that I'm feeling down. I just feel so deserted on this earth, left solely to fend for whatever ounce of optimism is left in me.

December 19th, 2022:

I abruptly sprung awake at 2 am to a heavy crashing sound, anxious about what awaited me downstairs. As I reached her room, I saw grandma accidentally spilling her water and cup on the floor. There was no ring from her necklace to wake me up, but the sound of the boisterous cup was enough to rouse me. I assisted her to the bathroom, although I admit I wasn't the most patient as I was still half-awake and panicked; it's hard to be 100% all of the time. She insisted on returning to bed independently, wanting to prove her independence. However, she just ended up sitting in bed with the lights on. She took two sleeping pills, which seemed to have the opposite effect on her. This isn't a regular occurrence, although it has happened before. I checked on her through the Blink cam and found her still sitting in bed, staring blankly with the lights on. I had to put her back in bed and turn off the lights. I couldn't leave her in that state and risk her getting out of bed alone. When I told her to lie down because the pills should have made her fall asleep, she laughed. I'm exhausted. It's almost 3 am, and all I want to do is cry. I feel overwhelming sadness for myself and her, as she can't truly comprehend what's happening. The line between patient and Grandma is nearly impossible to distinguish at times.

December 21st, 2022:

Today was an incredibly challenging day for me. Grandma had an accident and fell while trying to use the bathroom on her own. As I entered the room, the scene was disheartening - she was sitting on the shower floor, located right directly across from the toilet, and I unfortunately stepped in some waste. It was a mess, and I felt terrible for her; seeing her like that was devastating. She must have felt so embarrassed and defeated. Over the past few years, she has often expressed a desire to be put in a home so I wouldn't have to deal with her anymore. I always reassure her that she is not a burden and that taking care of her is my priority. Not only is it my priority, but it's my calling. The situation overwhelmed me to the point of becoming physically ill. I wish I was better at this. Trying to lift her proved challenging due to my back injury and her lack of muscle strength. Over the past few years of heavy lifting and excessive exercise, I've developed herniated discs in my back. Both of our bodies are deteriorating. I blame myself for not handling the lifting properly, as my back can't perform these tasks as I once could, leaving me feeling inadequate in my role. I call out for mom to help, and she then assists me in getting her up, cleaned, and back to bed safely. My mother tries to reassure me that it's not my fault and that I'm doing a great job, but I find it impossible to believe sometimes. Despite the difficulties, my grandma never fails to express her gratitude and tell me how great I am. She knows how hard I'm trying, and even in these toughest moments, I am so thankful that I'm the one here for her and not some stranger in a facility.

December 25th, 2022:

Christmas is here once again. My first thought was how fortunate we were to make it to this point. I knew I had to do something special for everyone. This could, and probably would, be our last holiday together. As much as that crushed my soul, I had to whip up some holiday cheer, even if it killed me. We managed to get grandma out into the living room for Christmas festivities, and as usual, we took turns opening her presents for her, as her hand had been fully clenched for some time now. The hand doctor previously explained that this is called "Dementia Clench Fist" and is a hand condition characterized by tight finger contractures. We keep a rolled-up gauze pad between her fingers and hand to prevent any cuts from her nails from occurring. I've often thought her clenched hand represents the anxiety and fear she must be experiencing. It's manifesting into a fist as if she's angry at the world for what happened to her. She would always complain of cold shoulders and kindly ask me to wrap a blanket around her, and I loved doing so. I loved making her feel warm and safe. One of her favorite gifts I got her was this half-blanket that went right over her shoulders, and it even had pockets for her tissues and Blistex, which she kept near her at all times. She was delighted by how practical this fancy blanket was, and instead of being delighted by her gratitude, I quickly became guilt-ridden because I hadn't thought of it earlier. I devised an idea for grandma's present to my mom a few weeks earlier. Grandma was able to recall memories from decades ago, so I thought of having her speak about my mother while I composed her thoughts into a poem. I would pose a question to her, and she would answer to the best of her ability. We obtained enough material to transform her message into a page-long, double-spaced scroll that I rolled to fit inside a small glass jar. It was like a message in a bottle, signifying thoughts that my grandma soon may be unable to recall, ensuring they will never be lost at "sea." I read aloud her loving message to her only daughter, my mother, and tears started streaming down my mom's face. It was such a beautiful moment between the two. My mom embraced grandma, and at that moment, I could see their mother-daughter bond as unreadable. Later on, we all feasted together, and I made grandma's favorite peanut butter fudge. I'd say it was a grand success.

December 31st, 2022:

Today is New Year's Eve, and I spent some time reflecting on the past year. I was looking forward to another year while also dreading my grandma's faster and steeper decline. I sat on her bed with her for a while, and we talked. I simply let her say whatever's on her mind while keeping her company. She just likes having someone there with her. I made her take photos with me because the dog was perfectly positioned between us, causing us both to crack up. My grandma and the dog often had conversations; she called her "Grandma's Good Girl," which was so sweet. My dog is never chatty with either my mom or me, yet whenever grandma would even say one word, she would start talking to her in a way I swear they knew what each other was saying. Sometimes, their "talking" would go on for at least ten minutes. I have countless video recordings of this, where you can hear my mom and I giggling, echoing in the background. My stomach would end up hurting from the guttural laughter.

January 6th, 2023:

We've decided to swap grandma's bed for a hospital bed, as she has now entered the hospice phase. Change is uncomfortable for her, especially with her advanced dementia and impaired vision. I tried placing a small Christmas tree on her dresser during the holidays, but she didn't like it. She had become accustomed to things being in certain places as it provided a sense of safety. We decided on the new bed because lifting her was increasingly strenuous, especially with her sleeping habits. It was also necessary for her safety, as the bed had side bars to prevent her from rolling off or having another fall by getting up during the night. However, she vehemently dislikes the new bed. Her immediate furrowed brow and irritated tone made it clear she was angered by it. I understand her frustration since she was used to her old bed and associated it with comfort. I can't shake this uneasy feeling about such a sudden change. The bed itself looks intimidating; fortunately, she can't see it, but it serves as a stark reminder of the reality of her condition and the involvement of hospice care. I had hoped the new bed would make things easier or better, but I see no positive aspect. The comfort and stability she had been accustomed to had been ripped from under her.

January 8th, 2023:

Today, my grandma had a distressing incident where she mistook her oxygen tank for the toilet and ended up soiling it. It breaks my heart to see her in this state, where she has lost control over her bodily functions. Each time an accident such as this occurs, I become terrified; she's falling apart, and her time clock is ticking faster. I can fathom why she has given up on many aspects of life. It's a heartbreaking process, and I can't blame her for feeling this way. I do everything in my power to cheer her up. The only positive aspect of her condition is that she will soon forget about this accident.

January 16th, 2023:

I often hear a couple of different sounds echoing in my head. The first is a faint uttering of "Nic.... Nic..." to which grandma would usually summon me to refill her water. On the other hand, she'd also nonchalantly call my name in the same manner when something more serious like a fall would occur. She would remain calm even when she was in utter need of assistance. She didn't want to feel as if she was troubling us, and I would vehemently insist that she should alert us for anything and that nothing she did was a bother. The other noise was the jingle her necklace would make when she rang for us. It almost sounded like an old Nokia text tone. There were many moments she would "ring" us, and by the time I got to her, she would have forgotten what she needed. We would usually laugh it off, turning these instances of memory lapse into a positive, and then I'd usually get her a snack. I received an urgent call from my grandma's pendant alarm at 4 am today, and though I was in a deep sleep, that sound always itched a part of my brain that made me instantly awake.

I knew it was urgent because she would never ring more than twice, especially consecutively and rapidly, leaving only a few seconds of silence between the jingles. By the end of the second ring, I was out of bed and running downstairs with a bulging pit in my stomach. As I neared the corner of her room, I felt an intensely catastrophic wave of emotion overtake me, and I was not ready for what awaited me. I found her on the floor, unable to move, with her head wedged under the bed. She was in excruciating pain. She informed me that she had been on the floor for an hour before reaching the pendant, as she had fallen on top of it, and it was too painful for her to move. I comforted her and asked what had happened, and she told me she had fallen and that her hip was in immense pain. I feel an overwhelming sense of guilt, picturing her helpless and lying on the floor, wondering if I could have prevented this if I had arrived sooner. My mother and I called an ambulance, and she was taken to the hospital while I stayed behind, caring for the animals, impatiently awaiting my turn to go to the hospital to see her. It was heart-wrenching to watch her being wheeled away, not knowing what was going to come next. Looking back at the video footage, I comprehend what went wrong. She had gotten up and reached for her dresser, which she would always use to guide her to the bathroom, but her dresser was further away than she had been used to. This was because her new hospital bed was narrower than her old one, leading her to miscalculate the distance she had once perfected. Throughout the day, I realized how mentally ill-equipped I was for the severity of the situation. I comforted her, apologizing for the circumstances, but deep down, I wished this hadn't happened more than anything. It was an out-of-body experience, and I was in shock. The fact that she had been on the ground for an hour before calling for help weighs heavily on me. The house feels torturous without her, even after just a few hours. Sleep became elusive as my mind was filled with regret. It became clear to me that the new bed was an awful idea.

January 17th, 2023:

Her condition has worsened, and she is barely responsive. A broken hip and shoulder were the prognosis, and the doctors concluded that since surgery wasn't an option, keeping her comfortable was all we could do. I was naive, and in my current state of shock, I figured she would somehow be able to heal and come home. Her hospital room is adorned with the number 821, her birthday. Ironically, this number represents both the beginning and end of her life. Not knowing how long I have left with her is eating away at me. I find myself desperately wishing for her bones to magically heal so that I can bring her back home.

Yesterday, when I asked my mother to be there when I first saw my grandma in the hospital, she lashed out at me and told me to act my age. Instead of that response, I hoped she would understand the meaning of family. It's not about age or maturity; it's about being there for each other during horrendous times. It was a heavy moment that revealed our family as fractured and hurting. I know it's her mom, and I can't imagine how she feels. We're all broken. I'm still in shock, and seeing her like this brings about a level of sadness I never knew existed. I can't stop crying.

January 18th, 2023:

She remains in the hospital, and her responsiveness has almost completely halted. A call I had with my uncle yesterday brought the realization that she may not come home, something that didn't even occur to me. I couldn't imagine her not coming back home. Her powerful presence fills our house, the main component that makes it a home. The weight of guilt is overwhelming. I have many regrets and wish I had done things differently. While she may not remember the details, I do, and that's what hurts the most. I should have spent more quality time with her, but the reality is that it became increasingly onerous as her condition deteriorated; to be submerged into this bottomless pit of degeneration felt like torture. When living in this caregiver reality, every waking moment is spent worrying, thinking, and caring for that person. Still, nothing is as torturous as having to accept your mind and body withdrawing from you while you're still alive. With tears streaming down my cheeks, I sit by her bedside, holding her fragile hand, never wanting to let go. I watch the sun fall behind the ocean as night falls, still clutching her hand. I've never seen a more exquisite and perfect sunset in my life.

January 19th, 2023:

My grandma's condition has reached its final stage, and she likely only has a few days left. Her body is shutting down, and the medical staff has decided to withhold water, providing only morphine drips for comfort. Witnessing her gradual decline is the most agonizing experience of my life. To bring her some solace throughout these days,

I've been reading her travel diaries aloud, knowing that somewhere deep down, she can hear me. I also put South Park on the TV, an homage to how she introduced me to this show as a child while she was living in New York. The big apple will always remind me of her. Attending the Macy's Day Parade, her teaching me how to hail a cab, stomping on the giant keyboard at FAO Schwartz, and blowing strawberry-flavored bubbles atop the rooftop party of her building during the 4th of July... these are all memories I will cherish for eternity. I share my love for her and reminisce about her incredible adventures throughout her life. Many years back, she gave me her beloved frog figurine collection that she's acquired throughout her many years of travel, and my room is showered in them. Each unique frog is from a different country and tells a different story. I long for the chance to discuss those memories with her once more. I tell her how greatly she impacted my life, how she is my greatest teacher, and how much I love her. My mother has been staying at the hospital overnight while I care for our animals at home. We alternate our time with her, spending most of the day with her. My sister also visits weekly, adding more familial support, which we desperately need. I hate leaving her at the hospital. The thought of her passing while I'm not there terrifies me. Nothing can prepare you for this kind of heartache.

January 20th, 2023:

Sitting by her bedside, endless thoughts consume me. The pain surrounding what was happening was far too great to grasp. My grandma was an extraordinary woman, and assuming the role of caregiver for her felt surreal. As time passed, it became increasingly taxing to grapple with the grief of losing someone who was still alive. Understanding the pain and frustration she endured, trapped within a mind and body that no longer functioned properly, was an agonizing process. I patiently listened to her retell the same stories and eagerly watched her excitement as she taught me the recipes she had shared countless times before. I treated her with dignity and kindness, my actions and words constantly reminding her that she was still human. She imparted valuable patience, humility, and resilience lessons throughout my life. She consistently expressed gratitude and offered kind words even at her lowest moments. Her advice never failed to resonate with me, and I will hold on to those words of wisdom forever. I ache for this nightmare to end for her. I cannot bear to witness her suffering any longer; this is the most inhumane type of suffering I could ever imagine. I wish it would end sooner. I watch the sunset with her again, admiring its beauty and power; it perfectly reflects the woman I am so lucky to call my grandma.

January 21st, 2023:

Grandma has passed away. I went to say my final goodbye alongside my mother and uncle. He flew in last night, barely dodging two snowstorms that had grounded all flights, and there is no doubt my grandma could sense his presence. She found peace knowing that she could go once he bid her farewell. Despite my mother's plea for me not to see her in her current state, I had already been witnessing it all week and felt compelled to give her one last hug. There was no way the

105

last time I said goodbye would be yesterday. It had to be today. These days at the hospital reminded me of how I would feel on Christmas each year, not knowing if it'd be the last.

I entered her room at around 11:00 am. Sensing that the end was near, my mother asked me to leave at 2:00 pm. Leaving her for the last time broke my heart into so many pieces I'm not sure it can ever be put back together. A couple of hours after I departed, she passed away with her children by her side. She knew it was time to go. Her life of mental anguish has finally come to an end. We loved having her here, but keeping her was selfish. She wanted to go, and she was ready to go. She hadn't been herself for a very long time. My grandma was the most brilliant and impressive woman I've ever known, and I can only hope to accomplish even a fraction of what she's done throughout her life. Wherever life may take me, I just want to make her proud. I'll keep our combined bucket list going; she'll be with me wherever I go. Having her with us these past four years has taught me more than I can comprehend, and I'm so thankful we had that time together. Home feels lonely without her, but I'm glad she's free now. I miss you every day, grandma. I love you.

March 4th, 2023:

A melodic tone that often cried wolf

Echoed for the end, unbeknownst

The room was engulfed in ruby-red

I, blind to see,

106

Unaware that my home ceased to be

She was lying there, fallen before me

Days stretched into eternities.

Yearning for your words,

Just one more time, an endearing plea

But the great unknown awaits

A once-living nightmare turned into endless dreams

Forever seeking you in slumber's realms

When my final day arrives, we'll meet at the beach

Observing the crashing waves together

A scene of pure serenity, how lovely it will be

Struggling to stay, yet longing to leave

Each day, grief we continued to weave

You, once vibrant like the calm before the storm

Until the clouds formed, your brilliance transformed

The plans for your departure are preordained

Oh, how I wish you could have remained

Now I sit here with thousands of tiny seeds

Nurturing what remains of you

Caring for them as I always used to

Watering my lush and lively garden

Planted by me

Made of you

Made in the USA
Columbia, SC
03 August 2024

f0a08927-1965-40c6-848d-c8e9b25a3067R01